My Early Life

Mohandas Karamchand Gandhi (1869–1948), revered as the 'Mahatma' and the 'Father of the Nation', was born in Porbandar, Gujarat. In the second half of the 1880s, Mohandas went to London to study law. After completing his education, he came back to India to work as a barrister. In 1893, he left for Natal in South Africa where he spent twenty-one years as an attorney, devoting himself to the cause of the Indians there against racial discrimination. On his final return to his Motherland in 1915, he joined the Indian National Congress and emerged as its pre-eminent leader, spearheading India's nonviolent movement for freedom from the British rule. His life and thoughts have inspired peaceful civil rights movements against oppression and for social change across the world.

Mahadev Desai (1892–1942), a freedom fighter and nationalist writer, was personal secretary to Mohandas Karamchand Gandhi. Associated with him from the year 1917 to 1942, Mahadev came to be known not only as a devoted disciple, but an outstanding interpreter of the mind of Mohandas. His works include translations from Tagore, twenty diaries, ten books, and the translation of *The Story of My Experiments with Truth* into English, among others. He also contributed articles for *Young India, Navjivan,* and *Harijanbandhu.*

Lalitha Zackariah is a noted Gandhi scholar and a former Director of the Research, Reference & Training Division of the Ministry of Information and Broadcasting, Government of India. She began her career with the office of The Collected Works of Mahatma Gandhi, where she served on the editorial staff for over twenty-five years. She is co-editor of the book *Together They Fought: Gandhi–Nehru Correspondence* (OUP 2011).

My Early Life

An illustrated Story

M.K. Gandhi

arranged and edited by
Mahadev Desai

annotated by
LALITHA ZACKARIAH

OXFORD
UNIVERSITY PRESS

OXFORD
UNIVERSITY PRESS

Oxford University Press is a department of the University of Oxford.
It furthers the University's objective of excellence in research, scholarship,
and education by publishing worldwide. Oxford is a registered trademark of
Oxford University Press in the UK and in certain other countries

Published in India by
Oxford University Press
2/11 Ground Floor, Ansari Road, Daryaganj, New Delhi 110 002, India

ISBN-13: 978-0-19-808379-5
ISBN-10: 0-19-808379-3

Typeset in Perpetua Std 13/19
by Eleven Arts, Keshav Puram, Delhi 110 035
Printed in India by Repro Knowledgecast Limited, Thane

Illustrations by Sourav Chatterjee

Contents

Publisher's Note

Much of the text of this book has been taken word for word from the two volumes of *The Story of My Experiments with Truth* (Navjivan Press, Ahmedabad, 1925 and 1929) and from *Satyagraha in South Africa* (S. Ganesan, Madras, 1928). Arranged and edited by Shri Mahadev Desai (1892–1942), who also rewrote certain parts, in collaboration with Gandhiji (1869–1948), the book was first published in 1932 by Oxford University Press under the title *My Early Life*.

My Early Life: An Illustrated Story is a new and revised edition of the book, conceived for the benefit of the young readers of today, who are distanced from the lifetime of Gandhiji by several decades.

It seeks to reanimate the author's written words, with illustrations and quotations from *The Collected Works of Mahatma Gandhi* (*CWMG*) interspersed in the text. These and the editorial annotations are in italics.

Foreword*

It was a happy thought of the Oxford University Press to arrange to publish an abridgment of Gandhiji's Autobiography for boys [children] in Indian schools. My help was sought, I being in touch with Gandhiji and being the translator of his Autobiography, in preparing the abridgment. I gladly consented. But I am not sure that the result does justice to the original, if only because the Autobiography, which is a model of condensation, nearly eludes condensation. But I ventured on the task thinking that there were some details and discussions of ethical and religious problems, in which young people may not be expected to be interested, and which might without detriment be omitted. Thus the narrative of the South African Satyagraha condensed from my friend Sjt. Valji Desai's translation of *The History of Satyagraha in South Africa*, omits intimate details of the South African Indians' problems and only retains episodes of permanent interest and perennial moral value.

* Reproduced from *My Early Life* originally published in 1932 by Oxford University Press India.

It was thought desirable that the abridgment should end with the year 1914. There was perhaps some justification for it. At any rate the omission of the portion dealing with the period since 1914 does not materially alter, for the student at school, the value of the Autobiography. All that the reader, however young, has heard of Gandhiji in recent years will be found in germ in what has gone before. The search for and devotion to truth—truth not only meaning veracity, but truth which is synonymous with God and hence is intimately linked with Love or Non-Injury—burns throughout the early period with a steady unflickering flame. The courage which one finds equal to grappling with mighty potentates and powers has its root in that sleepless devotion to truth which cannot be lived without love; the courage which thus becomes sacred and makes him, in Emerson's language, 'everywhere a liberator, but of a freedom that is ideal. ... free to speak truth, not free to lie', free to serve, not free to exploit, free to sacrifice himself, but not free to kill or injure—that sacred courage will be found in an ample measure even in the period before 1914.

'I am not writing the Autobiography to please critics', says the author in the second volume. 'Writing it is itself one of the experiments with truth. One of its objects is certainly to provide some comfort and food for reflection for my co-workers.'

Let me add that 'co-workers' in this excerpt means not necessarily those who are labelled *Satyagrahis*, but the circle embraces the whole confraternity which holds truth and non-violence sacred and who for the sake of them will forsake all. To my mind the youth are, or should be, naturally the first members of that confraternity. May this abridgment serve to whet their appetite to read the whole, in the original if possible.

MAHADEV DESAI
April 1932

Childhood

My father Kaba Gandhi never had any ambition to accumulate riches and left us very little property.

He had no education, save that of experience. At best, he may be said to have read up to the fifth Gujarati standard. Of history and geography he was innocent. But his rich experience of practical affairs stood him in good stead in the solution of the most intricate questions and in managing hundreds of men. Of religious training he had very little, but he had that kind of religious culture which frequent visits to temples and listening to religious discourses make available to many Hindus. In his last days he began reading the Gita at the instance of a learned Brahman friend of the family, and he used to repeat aloud some verses every day at the time of worship.

My father was a lover of his clan, truthful, brave and generous, but short-tempered. He was incorruptible and had earned a name for strict impartiality in his family as well as outside. His loyalty to the State of Rajkot, of which he was for some time Prime Minister, was well-known. An Assistant Political Agent spoke insultingly of the Rajkot Thakore Saheb, his chief, and he stood up to the insult. The Agent was angry and asked Kaba Gandhi to apologize. This he refused to do and was therefore kept under detention for a few hours. But when the Agent saw that Kaba Gandhi was adamant he ordered him to be released.

The outstanding impression my mother has left on my memory is that of saintliness. She was deeply religious. She would not think of taking her meals without her daily prayers. Going to the haveli—the Vaishnava temple—was one of her daily duties. As far as my memory can go back, I do not remember her having ever missed the *chaturmas*. She would take the hardest vows and keep them without flinching. Illness was no excuse for relaxing them. I can recall her once falling ill when she was observing the *chandrayan* vow, but the illness was not allowed to interrupt the observance. To keep two or three consecutive fasts was nothing to her. Living on one meal a day during chaturmas was a habit with her. Not content with that she fasted every alternate day during one chaturmas. During another chaturmas she vowed not to have food without seeing the sun. We children on those days would stand, staring at the sky, waiting to announce the appearance of the sun to our mother. Everyone knows that at the height of the rainy season the sun often does not condescend to show his face. And I remember days when, at his sudden appearance, we would rush and announce it to her. She would run out to see the sun, but by that time the fugitive would be gone, thus depriving her of her meal. 'That does not matter,' she would say cheerfully, 'God did not want me to eat today.' And then she would return to her round of duties.

My mother had strong common sense. She was well informed about matters of state, and ladies of the court thought highly of her intelligence. Often I would accompany her, exercising the privilege of childhood, and I still remember many lively discussions she had with the widowed mother of the Thakore Saheb.

Of these parents I was born at Porbandar (Kathiawad), otherwise known as Sudamapuri, on 2 October 1869.

> *Gandhiji often cited the example of Sudama of mythology to illustrate his point about humility, equality, and true love.*
>
> *Sudama and Krishna, disciples of the same Guru, Sandipani, were friends. Sudama had a large family and was very poor. His wife chided him for his other-worldliness and persuaded him to go to Krishna for help. Yet, once in the presence of the Lord, he forgot to ask for help. But when he returned home, he found it transformed by riches.*
>
> *'...kiddies, tell me, how was Sudama dressed when he went to Lord Krishna? Had he put on a dhoti with a silken border, or a coat of lace or a jolly flat Maharashtrian pugree and a scarf of brocade? Oh, no! He was only in rags ... 'Here, Rukhi, do you know what Sudama had on? You may not, but I do, for I was born in Porbandar, the home of Sudama. Well, then, which way was Sudama facing? Homewards? Brother dear, he had left his home and was making his way to where the Lord dwelt.'*
>
> *(The Collected Works of Mahatma Gandhi [CWMG], Vol. 15, p. 51)*

I passed my childhood in Porbandar. I recollect having been put to school. It was with some difficulty that I got through the multiplication tables. The fact that I recollect nothing more of those days than of having learnt, in company with other boys, to abuse our teacher, would strongly suggest that my intellect must have been sluggish, and my memory raw.

At School

I must have been about seven when my father left Porbandar for Rajkot to become a member of the Rajasthanik Court. There I was put into a primary school, and I can well recollect those days, including the names and other particulars of the teachers who taught me. As at Porbandar, so here, there was hardly anything to note about my studies. I could only have been a mediocre student. From this school I went to the suburban school and thence to the High School, having already reached my twelfth year. I do not remember having ever told a lie during this short period, either to my teachers or to my schoolmates. I used to be very shy and avoided all company. My books and my lessons were my sole companions. To be at school at the stroke of the hour and to run back home as soon as the school closed—that was my daily habit. I literally ran back, because I could not bear to talk to anybody. I was even afraid lest anyone should poke fun at me.

There is an incident which occurred at an examination during my first year at the High School, which is worth recording. Mr Giles, the Educational Inspector, had come on a visit of inspection. He had set us five words to write as a spelling exercise. One of the words was 'kettle'. I had misspelt it. The teacher tried to prompt me with the point of his boot, but I would not be prompted. It was beyond me to see that he wanted me to copy the spelling from my neighbour's slate, for I thought that the teacher was there to supervise us against copying. The result was that all the boys, except myself, were found to have spelt each word correctly. Only I had been stupid. The teacher tried later to bring this stupidity home to me, but without effect. I never could learn the art of 'copying'.

Yet the incident did not in the least diminish my respect for my teacher. I was by nature blind to the faults of elders. Later I came to know of many other failings of this teacher, but my regard for him remained the same. For I had learnt to carry out the orders of elders, not to scan their actions.

Two other incidents belonging to the same period have always clung to my memory. As a rule I had a distaste for any reading, beyond my school books. The daily lessons had to be done, because I disliked being taken to task by my teacher as much as I disliked deceiving him. Therefore I would do the lessons, but often without my mind on them. Thus when even the lessons could not be done properly, there was of course no question of any extra reading. But somehow my eyes fell on a book purchased by my father. It was *Shravana Pitribhakti Nataka* (a play about Shravana's devotion to his parents). I read it with intense interest. There came

to our place about the same time itinerant showmen. One of the pictures
I was shown was of Shravana carrying his blind parents on a pilgrimage.
The book and the picture left an indelible impression on my mind. 'Here
is an example for you to copy,' I said to myself. The agonized lament of the
parents over Shravana's death is still fresh in my memory.

> Shravana, of the Ramayana, was a devoted son, who carried his blind parents to various
> places of pilgrimage in baskets put in a sling attached to two ends of a pole. While fetching
> water from a river, he was killed by King Dasharatha, who mistook the sound of water
> filling the pitcher for an elephant drinking.

The melting tune moved me deeply and I played it on a concertina which my
father had bought for me.

There was a similar incident connected with another play. Just about this
time, I had secured my father's permission to see a play performed by a
certain dramatic company. This play—*Harischandra*—captured my heart.
I could never be tired of seeing it. But how often should I be permitted
to go? It haunted me and I must have acted *Harischandra* to myself times
without number. 'Why should not all be truthful like Harischandra?' was the
question I asked myself day and night. To follow truth and to go through all
the ordeals Harischandra went through was the one ideal it inspired in me.
I literally believed in the story of Harischandra. The thought of it all often
made me weep. My common sense tells me today that Harischandra could
not have been a historical character. But for me, both Harischandra and
Shravana are living realities and I am sure I should be touched as before if I
were to read again those plays today.

I was not regarded as a dunce at the High School. I always enjoyed the
affection of my teachers. Certificates of progress and character used to be
sent to the parents every year. I never had a bad certificate. In fact, I even
won prizes after I passed out of the second standard. In the fifth and sixth
I obtained scholarships of rupees four and ten respectively, an achievement

for which I have to thank good luck more than my own merit. For the scholarships were not open to all, but reserved for the best boys amongst those coming from the Sorath Division of Kathiawad. And in those days there could not have been many boys from Sorath in a class of forty to fifty.

My own recollection is that I had not any high regard for my ability. I used to be astonished whenever I won prizes and scholarships. But I very jealously guarded my character. The least little blemish drew tears from my eyes. When I merited, or seemed to the teacher to merit, a rebuke, it was unbearable for me. I remember having once received corporal punishment. I did not so much mind the punishment, as the fact that it was considered my desert. I wept piteously. That was when I was in the first or second standard. There was another such incident during the time when I was in the seventh standard. Dorabji Edulji Gimi was the headmaster then. He was popular among the boys, though he was a disciplinarian. He was a man of method and a good teacher. He had made gymnastics and cricket compulsory for the boys of the upper standards. I disliked both. I never took part in any exercise, cricket or football, before they were made compulsory. My shyness was one of the reasons for this aloofness, which I now see was wrong. I then had the false notion that gymnastics had nothing to do with education. Today I know that physical training should have as much place in the curriculum as mental training.

I may mention, however, that I was none the worse for abstaining from exercise. That was because I had read in books about the benefits of long walks in the open air, and having liked the advice, I had formed a habit of taking walks, which has still remained with me. These walks gave me a fairly hardy constitution.

> '...We are as careless about exercise as about diet. To stroll one or two miles at a leisurely pace is no exercise. To hit a billiard ball one or two hundred times with a cue is also no exercise. When exercise is taken in this manner in a room full of foul-smelling air, the effect

is bound to be harmful. In our predicament, when no other form of exercise is convenient, walking is the best exercise. But exercise is worth the name only if one can walk six miles at a stretch in the morning and again in the evening. The walking should be done briskly, at a speed of four miles an hour.'

(*CWMG, Vol. 13, p. 270*)

But though I was none the worse for having neglected exercise, I am still paying the penalty of another neglect. I do not know whence I got the

notion that good handwriting was not a necessary part of education, but I retained it until I went to England: I then saw that bad handwriting should be regarded as a sign of an imperfect education. Let every young man and woman understand that good handwriting is a necessary part of education.

'Bad handwriting is a serious defect. A good hand is an accomplishment. By writing a bad hand, we place a heavy burden on our friends and elders and harm our work.'

(CWMG, Vol. 15, p. 98)

'I know very few whose writing is worse than mine, and yet because of my dislike of typewriters, if I could possibly write with my own hand, I will inflict that illegible hand in preference to having my letters typed or typing them myself... Typewriting certainly results in economy of time. But whilst I admit that time is money, I do not admit that money is everything ... And the inroads the typewriter is making have all but destroyed the magnificent art of calligraphy.'

(CWMG, Vol. 33, pp. 396–7)

Two more reminiscences of my school days are worth recording. English became the medium of instruction in most subjects from the fourth standard. I found myself completely at sea. Geometry was a new subject in which I was not particularly strong and the English medium made it still more difficult for me. The teacher was efficient enough, but I could not follow him. When, however, with effort I reached the thirteenth proposition of Euclid, the utter simplicity of the subject was suddenly revealed to me. A subject which only required a pure and simple use of one's reasoning powers could not be difficult. Ever since that time Geometry has been both easy and interesting for me.

Sanskrit, however, proved a harder task. In Geometry there was nothing to memorize, whereas in Sanskrit, I thought, everything had to be learnt by heart. This subject also commenced from the fourth standard. As soon as I entered the sixth I became disheartened. The teacher was a hard taskmaster, anxious, as I thought, to force the boys. There was a sort of rivalry going on between the Sanskrit and the Persian teachers. The Persian teacher was lenient. It was common talk amongst us boys that Persian was very easy and the Persian teacher very good and considerate to the students. The 'easiness' tempted me and one day I sat in the Persian class. The Sanskrit teacher was grieved. He called me to his side and said: 'How can you forget that you are the son of a Vaishnava father? Won't you learn the language of your own religion? If you have any difficulty, why not come to me? I want to teach you students Sanskrit to the best of my ability. As you proceed further, you will find in it things of absorbing interest. You should not lose heart. Come and sit again in the Sanskrit class'.

This kindness melted me. I could not disregard the teacher's affection. Today, I cannot but think with gratitude of Krishnashankar Pandya. For if I had not acquired the little Sanskrit that I learnt then, I should have found it difficult to take any interest in our sacred books. In fact I deeply regret that I was not able to acquire a more thorough knowledge of the language, because I have since realized that every Hindu boy and girl should possess sound Sanskrit learning.

It is now my opinion that in all Indian curricula of higher education there should be a place for Hindi, Sanskrit, Persian, Arabic and English, the vernacular being the medium of instruction. This big list need not frighten anyone. If our education were more systematic, and the boys free from the burden of having to learn their subjects through a foreign medium, I am sure learning many languages would not be an irksome task, but a pleasure.

> 'Education through a foreign language entails an excessive strain which only our boys could bear; they must need pay dearly for it, though. To a large extent, they lose the capacity of shouldering any other burden afterwards. Our graduates, therefore, are a useless lot, weak of body, without any zest for work, and mere imitators. They suffer an atrophy of the creative faculty and of the capacity for original thinking, and grow up without a spirit of enterprise and the qualities of perseverance, courage and fearlessness.'

(CWMG, Vol. 14, pp. 14–15)

A scientific knowledge of one language makes knowledge of other languages comparatively easy.

In reality, Hindi, Gujarati and Sanskrit may be regarded as one language, and Persian and Arabic also as one. Though Persian belongs to the Aryan, and Arabic to the Semitic family of languages, there is a close relationship between Persian and Arabic, because both claim their full growth through the rise of Islam. Urdu I have not regarded as a distinct language, because it has adopted the Hindi grammar, and its vocabulary is mainly Persian and Arabic, and he who would learn good Urdu must learn Persian and Arabic, as one who would learn good Gujarati, Hindi, Bengali, or Marathi, must learn Sanskrit.

Marriage and Meat-eating

It is my painful duty to have to record here my marriage at the age of thirteen. As I see youngsters of the same age about me, who are under my care, and think of my own marriage, I am inclined to pity myself and congratulate them on having escaped my lot. I can see no moral argument in support of such a preposterously early marriage. I was still at the High School when I was married. Only in our present Hindu society do studies and marriage go thus hand in hand.

Another painful thing to record here is my falling in with evil company, which I regard as a tragedy in my life.

This companion was originally my elder brother's friend. They were classmates. I knew the companion's weaknesses, but I regarded him as a faithful friend. My mother, my eldest brother, and my wife warned me that I was in bad company. I was too proud a husband to heed my wife's warning. But I dared not go against the opinion of my mother and my eldest brother. Nevertheless I pleaded with them saying that I knew his weaknesses, but that I also knew his virtues, and that I expected to reform him.

I do not think this satisfied them, but they accepted my explanation and let me go my way.

I have seen since that I had calculated wrongly. A reformer cannot afford to have close intimacy with him whom he seeks to reform. True friendship is an identity of souls rarely to be found in this world. Only between like natures can friendship be worthy and enduring. Friends react on one another. Hence, in friendship, there is very little scope for reform. I am of opinion that all exclusive intimacies are to be avoided; for man far more readily takes in vice than virtue. And he who would be friends with God must remain alone, or make the whole world his friend. I may be wrong, but my effort to cultivate an intimate friendship proved a failure.

A wave of 'reform' was sweeping over Rajkot at the time when I first came across this friend. He informed me that many of our teachers were secretly taking meat and wine. He also named many well-known people of Rajkot as belonging to the same company. There were also, I was told, some High School boys among them.

I was surprised and pained. I asked my friend the reason and he explained it thus: 'We are a weak people because we do not eat meat. The English are able to rule over us, because they are meat-eaters. You know how hardy I am, and a great runner too. It is because I am a meat-eater. Meat-eaters do not have boils or tumours, and even if they sometimes happen to have any, they heal quickly. Our teachers and other distinguished people who eat meat are no fools. They know its virtues. You should do likewise. There is nothing like trying. Try, and see what strength it gives you'.

All these pleas on behalf of meat-eating were not advanced at a single sitting. They represent the substance of a long and elaborate argument which my friend was trying to impress upon me from time to time. My elder brother had already fallen. He therefore supported my friend's argument. I certainly looked feeble-bodied by the side of my brother and this friend. They were both hardier, physically stronger and more daring. This friend's exploits cast a spell over me. He could run long distances and extraordinarily fast. He was an adept in high and long jumping. He could put up with any amount of corporal punishment. He would often display his exploits to me; and as one is always dazzled when he sees in others the qualities that he lacks himself, I was dazzled by this friend's exploits. This was followed by a strong desire to be like him. I could hardly jump or run. Why should not I also be as strong as he?

Again I was a coward. I used to be haunted by the fear of thieves, ghosts and serpents. I did not dare to stir out of doors at night. Darkness was a terror to me. It was almost impossible for me to sleep in the dark, as I would imagine ghosts coming from one direction, thieves from another and serpents from a third. I could not therefore bear to sleep without a light in the room. How could I disclose my fears to the wife sleeping by my side, now at the threshold of youth? I knew that she had more courage than I, and I felt ashamed of myself. She knew no fear of serpents and ghosts. She could go out anywhere in the dark. My friend knew all these weaknesses of mine. He would tell me that he could hold in his hand live serpents, could defy thieves and had no belief in ghosts. And all this was, of course, the result of eating meat.

A doggerel of Narmad, the Gujarati poet, was in vogue amongst us schoolboys, as follows:

> Behold the mighty Englishman
> He rules the Indian small,
> Because being a meat-eater
> He is five cubits tall.

All this had its due effect on me. I was beaten. It began to grow on me that meat-eating was good, that it would make me strong and daring, and that if the whole country took to meat-eating the English could be overcome.

A day was thereupon fixed for beginning the experiment. It had to be conducted in secret as my parents were staunch Vaishnavas, and I was extremely devoted to them. I knew that the moment they came to know of my having eaten meat, they would be grievously shocked. Moreover, my love of truth made me extra cautious. I cannot say that I did not know then that I should have to deceive my parents if I began eating meat. But my mind was bent on the 'reform'. It was not a question of pleasing the palate. I did not know whether it was palatable. I wished to be strong and daring and wanted my countrymen also to be such, so that we might defeat the English and make India free. The word '*swaraj*' I had not yet heard. But I knew what freedom meant. The frenzy of the 'reform' blinded me. And having ensured secrecy, I falsely persuaded myself that mere hiding of the deed from parents was no departure from truth.

So the day came. It is difficult fully to describe my condition. There was, on the one hand, the zeal for 'reform', and the novelty of making a momentous departure in life. There was, on the other, the shame of hiding like a thief the very thing I was so keen on doing. I cannot say which of the two swayed me most. We went in search of a lonely spot by the river, and there I saw for the first time in my life—meat. There was baker's bread also. I relished neither. The goat's meat was as tough as leather. I simply could not eat it. I was sick and had to leave off eating.

Gandhiji went to Europe in 1931 to attend the Second Round Table Conference. He travelled to France during this period. At Lausanne, answering a question at a meeting about the value of a vegetarian diet, he said:

'Priceless values for me, not for beef-eating Europe. But I do feel that spiritual progress does demand at some stage—an inexorable demand—that we should cease to kill our fellow creatures for satisfaction of our bodily wants. The beautiful lines of Goldsmith occur to me as I tell you of my vegetarian fad:

*"No flocks that range the valley free
To slaughter I condemn;
Taught by the Power that pities me
I learn to pity them."'*

(CWMG, Vol. 48, p. 408)

☞

The goat in fact became dear to Gandhiji, who had taken to drinking goat's milk for some time. There were two goats at his ashram in Ahmadabad for the purpose, inspiring Gandhiji to jest in a letter of 1919 to his son Devdas:

'Rasiklal Harilal Mohandas Gandhi,
Had a goat in his keeping:
The goat would not be milked
And Gandhi would not stop his weeping.'

(CWMG, Vol. 15, p. 100)

☞

Here is an excerpt from an article by one of Gandhiji's co-workers, Yusuf Meherally:
'Almost the first question that an Indian is asked in a foreign country is about Gandhi. In 1938, I happened to be travelling from New York to Mexico by car. At the wayside service station, the car halted for supplies. The attendant, scanning my Indian costume with interest for a while, could restrain himself no longer.

"What country do you come from?"
"India," I replied.
"India, eh? How is good old Gandhi?"
"Fine."
"Is he still fasting?"
"Sure."
"How's the goat?"
"Going strong."'

I had a very bad night afterwards. A horrible nightmare haunted me. Every time I dropped off to sleep it would seem as though a live goat were bleating inside me, and I would jump up full of remorse. But then I would remind myself that meat-eating was a duty and so take heart.

In the Wake of
Evil Company

My friend was not a man to give in easily. He now began to cook various delicacies with meat, and dress them neatly. And for dining, no longer the secluded spot on the river was chosen, but a State house, with its dining hall, and tables and chairs, about which my friend had made arrangements in collusion with the chief cook there.

This bait had its effect. I got over my dislike for bread, forswore my compassion for the goats, and became a relisher of meat-dishes, if not of meat itself. This went on for about a year. But not more than half a dozen meat-feasts were enjoyed in all; because the State house was not available every day, and there was the obvious difficulty about preparing frequently expensive savoury meat dishes. I had no money to pay for this 'reform'. My friend had therefore always to find the wherewithal. I had no knowledge where he found it, but find it he did, because he was bent on turning me into a meat-eater. But even his means must have been limited, and hence these feasts had necessarily to be few and far between.

Whenever I had occasion to indulge in these surreptitious feasts, dinner at home was out of the question. My mother would naturally ask me to take my food and want to know the reason why I did not wish to eat. I would say to her, 'I have no appetite today; there is something wrong with my digestion'. It was not without compunction that I devised these pretexts. I knew I was lying, and that too to my mother. I also knew that if my mother and father came to know of my having become a meat-eater, they would be deeply shocked. This knowledge was gnawing at my heart.

Therefore I said to myself: 'Though it is essential to eat meat, and also essential to take up food "reform" in the country, yet deceiving one's parents is worse than eating meat. In their lifetime, therefore, meat-eating must be out of the question. When they are no more and when I have found my freedom, I might eat meat openly, but until that moment arrives I must abstain from it.'

This decision I communicated to my friend, and I have never since gone back to meat. My parents never knew that two of their sons had become meat-eaters.

I abjured meat out of the purity of my desire not to lie to my parents, but I did not abjure the company of my friend. My zeal for reforming him had proved disastrous for me, and all the time I was completely unconscious of the fact.

The same company would have led me into faithlessness to my wife. But I was saved by the skin of my teeth. I went into the jaws of sin, but God in His infinite mercy, protected me against myself. Even this was far from opening my eyes to the undesirability of this company. I, therefore had many more bitter draughts in store for me, until later in life my eyes were actually opened by an ocular demonstration of some of his lapses quite unexpected by me.

One thing I must mention now, as it pertains to the same period. I had differences with my wife. One of the reasons was undoubtedly the company of this friend. I was a devoted but a jealous husband, and this friend fanned the flame of my suspicions about my wife. I never could doubt his veracity. And I have never forgiven myself the violence of which I have been guilty in often having pained my wife by acting on his information. Only a Hindu wife tolerates the torment caused by suspicious husbands, and that is why I have regarded woman as an incarnation of tolerance. A servant wrongly suspected may throw up his job, a son may leave his father's roof, and a friend may put an end to the friendship. The wife, if she suspects her husband, will harbour secret grief, but if the husband suspects her, she is doomed. Where is she to go? Divorce is not generally open to a Hindu wife. Law has no remedy for her. I can never forget or forgive myself for having tortured my wife with baseless suspicions.

The canker of suspicion was rooted out only when I understood *ahimsa* in all its bearings. I saw then the glory of *brahmacharya* and realized that the wife is not the husband's bonded slave, but his companion and his helpmate, and an equal partner in all his joys and sorrows—as free as the husband to choose her own path.

> 'I have been touring all over India since 1915 and saying everywhere that, till a woman takes her place by the side of man and claims her rights, she will not come into her own. And till she does so, there can be no progress for us. If one of the two wheels of a carriage remains in working condition but the other goes out of order, the carriage will not run properly.'
>
> (CWMG, Vol. 15, p. 49)

> 'There is not the slightest doubt that wives have all the rights which the husbands enjoy. Their duties are different but their rights are the same. If a woman sets out in shirts and trousers with a gun in her hand, a man has no right to stop her. In such matters men and women enjoy equal rights...'

'...The husband saying, "I am your master, you are my property, you should do as I tell you" is the kind of thing that has no place in my ideology. Satyagraha is the final weapon against such an attitude in husbands ...'

(CWMG, Vol. 61, p. 123)

❧

'I have included service of women in the constructive programme, for though satyagraha has automatically brought India's women out from their darkness as nothing else could have in such an incredibly short period of time, Congressmen have not felt the call to see that women become equal partners in the fight for swaraj. They have not realized that woman must be the true helpmate of man in the mission of service. Woman has been suppressed under custom and law for which man was responsible and in the shaping of which she had no hand. In a plan of life based on non-violence, woman has as much right to shape her own destiny as man has to shape his.'

(CWMG, Vol. 75, p. 155)

Whenever I think of those dark days of doubts and suspicions, I am filled with loathing at my folly and my lustful cruelty, and I deplore my blind devotion to my friend.

The Story of a Confession

I have still to relate some of my failings during this meat-eating period and also previous to it, which date from before my marriage or soon after.

A relative and I once developed a desire for smoking. Not that we saw any good in it, or were enamoured of the smell of a bidi. We simply imagined a sort of pleasure in emitting clouds of smoke from our mouths. My uncle had the habit, and when we saw him smoking, we thought we should copy his example. But we had no money. So we began pilfering stumps of bidis thrown away by my uncle.

The stumps, however, were not always available, and could not give much smoke either. So we began to steal coppers from the servant's pocket-money in order to purchase bidis. Then the question was where to keep them. We could not of course smoke in the presence of elders. We managed somehow for a few weeks on these stolen coppers. In the meantime we heard that the stalks of a certain plant were porous and could be smoked like cigarettes. We got them and began puffing them.

But we were far from being satisfied with such things as these. Our want of independence began to smart. It was unbearable that we should be unable to do anything without the elders' permission. At last, in sheer disgust, we decided to commit suicide!

But how were we to do it? From where were we to get the poison? We had heard that *dhatura* seeds were an effective poison. Off we went to the jungle in search of these seeds, and got them. Evening was thought to be the auspicious hour. We went to the Kedarji Mandir, put ghee in the temple-lamp, had *darshan* and then looked for a lonely corner. But our courage failed us. Supposing we were not instantly killed? And what was the good of killing ourselves? Why not rather put up with the lack of independence? Nevertheless we swallowed two or three seeds. We dared not take more. We found ourselves too cowardly to face death, and decided to go to the Ramji Mandir to compose ourselves, and to dismiss the thought of suicide.

I realized that it was not as easy to commit suicide as to contemplate it. And since then threats to commit suicide have not perturbed me much.

The thought of suicide ultimately resulted in both of us bidding goodbye to the habit of smoking stumps of bidis and of stealing the servant's coppers for the purpose.

The desire to smoke has never come back to me. On the contrary I have come to regard the habit of smoking as barbarous, dirty and harmful. I have never understood why there is such a rage for smoking throughout the world. It is unbearable to me to travel in a compartment full of people smoking. I get choked.

> *Writing later about the baneful effects of smoking, Gandhiji observed in* General Knowledge about Health:
>
> *'Smoking weakens the digestion, renders food tasteless so that more and more spices have to be added to it. The smoker's breath is offensive. The smoke that he exhales pollutes the atmosphere. At times, he gets small ulcers in his mouth. Gums and teeth become black or yellow, and some persons have contracted serious diseases in consequence. It seems strange that people who disapprove of drinking see nothing wrong in smoking; when, however we remember how subtle is the poison of smoking, we easily see enough why it is that men who hate alcohol are nevertheless ready to enjoy smoking. Those who wish to remain healthy should definitely give up the cigarette.'*
>
> (CWMG, Vol.11, p. 481)

But this smoking and the pilfering to which it led might be considered excusable compared to what I was to be drawn into a few years later. I pilfered the coppers when I was twelve or thirteen, possibly less. The other theft was committed when I was fifteen. In this case I stole a bit of gold out of my meat-eating brother's armlet. This brother had run into a debt of about twenty-five rupees. He had on his arm an armlet of solid gold. It was not difficult to clip a bit out of it.

Well, it was done, and the debt cleared. But this was more than I could bear. I resolved never to steal again. I also made up my mind to confess it to my father. But I had not the courage to speak to him. Not that I was afraid of my father beating me. I do not recall his ever having beaten any of us. I was afraid of the pain that the confession would cause him. But I felt that the risk had to be taken; that there could not be a cleansing without a clean confession.

I decided at last to write out the confession, to submit it to my father, and ask his forgiveness. In this note not only did I confess my guilt, but I asked adequate punishment for it, and closed with a request to him to not punish himself for my offence. I also pledged never to repeat the sin.

I was trembling as I handed the confession to my father. He was then lying on a sickbed. His bedstead was a plain wooden plank. I handed him the note and awaited my doom.

He read it through and pearl-drops trickled down his cheeks wetting the paper. For a moment he closed his eyes in thought and then tore up the note. He had sat up to read it. He lay down. I wept with him. I could see my father's agony. If I were a painter I could draw a picture of the whole scene today, it is still so vivid in my mind.

Those pearl-drops of love cleansed my heart, and washed my sin away. Only he who has experienced such love can know what it is. As the hymn says:

> Only he
> Who is smitten with the arrows of love,
> Knows its power.

Looking back upon it, the scene was an object-lesson in ahimsa, although then I could read in it nothing more than a father's love. When such ahimsa becomes all-embracing, it transforms everything it touches. There is no limit to its power.

> 'Literally speaking, ahimsa means non-killing. But to me, it has a world of meaning and takes me into realms much higher, infinitely higher, than the realm to which I would go, if I merely understood by ahimsa non-killing. Ahimsa really means that you may not offend anybody, you may not harbour an uncharitable thought even in connection with one who may consider himself to be your enemy. ...For one who follows the doctrine of ahimsa, there is no room for an enemy; he denies the existence of an enemy. But there are people who consider themselves to be his enemies, and he cannot help that circumstance. So, it is held that we may not harbour an evil thought even in connection with such persons. If we return blow for blow, we depart from the doctrine of ahimsa. ...If you express your love—ahimsa—in such a manner that it impresses itself indelibly upon your so-called enemy, he must return that love.'
>
> (CWMG, Vol. 13, pp. 228–9)

This sort of sublime forgiveness was not natural to my father. I had thought that he would be angry, say hard things, and strike his forehead. But he was so wonderfully peaceful, and I believe this was due to my clean confession. A clean confession, combined with a promise never to commit the sin again, when offered before one who has the right to receive it, is the purest type of repentance. I know that my confession made my father feel absolutely safe about me, and increased his affection for me beyond measure.

A Double Shame

The time of which I am now speaking would be my sixteenth year. My father, as we have seen, was bedridden. My mother, an old servant of the house, and I were his principal attendants. I had the duties of a nurse, which mainly consisted in dressing the wound, giving him his medicine, and compounding drugs whenever they had to be made up at home. Every night I massaged his legs and retired only when he asked me to do so or after he had fallen asleep. I loved to do this service. I do not remember ever having neglected it. All the time at my disposal, after performing the daily duties, was divided between school and attending on my father. I would only go out for an evening walk either when he could spare me or when he was feeling well.

This was also the time when my wife was expecting a baby, a circumstance which, as I can see today, meant a double shame for me. For one thing I did not restrain myself, as I should have done, whilst I was yet a student. And secondly, this carnal lust got the better of what I regarded as my duty to study, and of what was even a greater duty, my devotion to my parents, Shravana having been my ideal since childhood. Every night whilst my hands were busy massaging my father's legs, my mind was hovering about my bedroom—and that too at a time when religion, medical science and common sense alike forbade sexual intercourse. I was always glad to be relieved from my duty, and went straight to the bedroom after doing obeisance to my father.

At the same time my father was getting worse every day. The dreadful night came. My uncle was then in Rajkot. I have a faint recollection that he had come to Rajkot having received the news that my father was sinking. The brothers were deeply attached to each other. My uncle would sit near my father's bed the whole day, and would insist on sleeping by his bedside after sending us all to sleep. No one had dreamt that this was to be the fateful night. The danger of course was there.

It was 10:30 or 11 p.m. I was giving the massage. My uncle offered to relieve me. I was glad and went straight to the bedroom. My wife, poor thing, was fast asleep. But how could she sleep when I was there? I woke her up. In five or six minutes, however, the servant knocked at the door. I startled. 'Get up,' he said, 'Father is very ill.' I knew of course that he was very ill, and so I guessed what 'very ill' meant at that moment. I sprang out of bed.

'What is the matter? Do tell me!'

'Father is no more.'

So all was over! I had but to wring my hands. I felt deeply ashamed and miserable. I ran to my father's room. I saw that if animal passion had not blinded me, I should have been spared the torture of separation from my father during his last moments. I should have been massaging him, and he would have died in my arms. But now it was my uncle who had had this honour. He was so deeply devoted to his elder brother, that he had earned the honour! My father had forebodings of the coming event. He had made a sign for pen and paper, and written: 'Prepare for the last rites'. He had then snapped the amulet off his arm, and also his gold necklace of tulsi-beads and flung them aside. A moment after this he was no more.

I have never been able to efface or forget the shame of having deserted for the satisfaction of carnal desire a dying father's bedside; and I have always thought, that although I was devoted to my parents and would have given up anything for them, yet when the devotion was weighed it was found unpardonably wanting. It took me long to free myself from the shackles of lust, and I had to pass through many ordeals before I could overcome it.

Before I close this chapter of my double shame, I may mention that the poor mite that was born to my wife scarcely breathed for more than three or four days. Nothing else could be expected.

A Guiding Principle

In Rajkot I got an early grounding in toleration for all branches of Hinduism and sister religions. For my father and mother would visit the *haveli* as also Shiva's and Rama's temples, and would take or send us youngsters there. Jain monks also would pay frequent visits to my father, and would even go out of their way to accept food from us—non-Jains. They would have talks with my father on subjects religious and mundane.

He had Mussalman and Parsi friends, who would talk to him about their own faiths, and he would listen to them always with respect, and often with interest. Being his nurse, I had many chances of being present during these talks. These many things combined to inculcate in me toleration for all faiths.

But the fact that I had learnt to be tolerant of other religions did not mean that I had any living faith in God. One thing, however, took deep root in me—the conviction that morality is the basis of things, and that truth is the substance of all morality. Truth became my sole objective. It began to grow in magnitude every day, and my conception of it also has been ever widening.

A Gujarati didactic stanza likewise gripped my mind and heart. Its precept—return good for evil—became my guiding principle. It became such a passion with me that I began numerous experiments in it. Here are those (for me) wonderful lines:

> For a bowl of water give a goodly meal;
> For a kindly greeting bow thou down with zeal;
> For a simple penny pay thou back with gold;
> If thy life be rescued, life do not withhold.
> Thus the words and actions of the wise regard;
> Every little service tenfold they reward.
> But the truly noble know all men as one,
> And return with gladness good for evil done.

The Triple Vow

I passed the matriculation examination in 1887. It then used to be held at two centres, Ahmedabad and Bombay. The general poverty of the country naturally led Kathiawad students to prefer the nearer and the cheaper centre, and the poverty of my family likewise dictated to me the same choice. This was my first journey anywhere without a companion.

My elders wanted me to pursue my studies at college after the matriculation. There was a college in Bhavnagar as well as in Bombay and as the former was cheaper, I decided to go there and join the Samaldas College. I went, but found myself entirely at sea. Everything was difficult. I could not follow, let alone take interest in, the professors' lectures. It was no fault of theirs. The professors in that college were regarded as first-rate. But I was so raw. At the end of the first term, I returned home.

We had in Mavji Dave, who was a shrewd and learned Brahman, an old friend and adviser of the family. He strongly advised my widowed mother to send me to England for three years so that I might become a barrister. He turned to me and asked: 'Would you not rather go to England than study here?' Nothing could have been more welcome to me. I was fighting shy of my difficult studies at college. So I jumped at the proposal and said that the sooner I was sent the better.

My elder brother was greatly exercised in his mind. How was he to find the wherewithal to send me? And was it proper to trust a young man like me to go abroad alone?

My mother was still more sorely perplexed. She did not like the idea of parting from me. She had begun making minute inquiries. Someone had told her that young men got lost in England. Someone else had said that they took to meat; and yet another that they could not live there without liquor. 'How about all this?' she asked me. I said: 'Will you not trust me? I shall not lie to you. I swear that I shall not touch any of those things. If there were any such danger, would Joshiji let me go?'

'I can trust you here in your natural surroundings,' she said. 'But how can I trust you in a distant land? I am dazed and know not what to do. I will ask Becharji Swami.'

Becharji Swami was originally a Modh Bania, but had now become a Jain monk. He too was a family adviser like Joshiji. He came to my help, and said: 'I shall get the boy solemnly to take the three vows, and then he can be allowed to go'. He administered the oath and I vowed not to touch wine, woman and meat. This done, my mother gave her permission.

The High School had a send-off in my honour. It was an uncommon thing for a young man of Rajkot to go to England. I had written out a few words of thanks. But I could scarcely stammer them out.

First Experiences
in England

I sailed from Bombay on 4 September 1888. I did not feel at all seasick. But as the days passed, I became nervous. I felt shy even speaking to the steward. I was quite unaccustomed to talking English, and except for Sjt. Mazmudar, all the other passengers in the second saloon seemed to be English. I could not speak to them. For I could rarely follow them when they came up to speak to me, and even when I understood them I could say nothing in reply. I had to frame every sentence in my mind, before I could bring it out. I was innocent of the use of knives and forks and had not the courage to inquire what dishes on the menu were free of meat. I therefore never took my meals at table but always had them in my cabin, and they consisted principally of sweets and fruits which I had brought with me. Sjt. Mazmudar had no difficulty, and he mixed with everybody. He would move about freely on the deck, while I hid myself in the cabin the whole day, only venturing up on the deck when there were but few people. Sjt. Mazmudar kept pleading with me to associate with the passengers and to talk with them freely. He told me that lawyers should have a long tongue, and related to me his legal experiences. He advised me to take every possible opportunity of talking in English, and not to mind making mistakes which were obviously unavoidable with a foreign tongue. But nothing could make me conquer my shyness.

An English passenger, taking kindly to me, drew me into conversation. He was older than I. He asked me what I ate, what I was, where I was going, why I was shy, and so on. He also advised me to come to the table. He laughed at my insistence on abjuring meat, and said in a friendly way when we were in the Red Sea: 'It is all very well so far but you will have to revise your decision in the Bay of Biscay. And it is so cold in England that one cannot possibly live there without meat.'

'But I have heard that people *can* live there without eating meat,' I said.

'Rest assured it is a fib,' said he. 'No one, to my knowledge, lives there, without being a meat-eater. Don't you see that I am not asking you to take liquor, though I do so? But I do think you should eat meat, for you cannot live without it.'

'I thank you for your kind advice, but I have solemnly promised my mother not to touch meat and therefore I cannot think of taking it. If it be found impossible to get on without it, I would far rather go back to India than eat meat in order to remain there.'

We entered the Bay of Biscay, but I did not feel the need either of meat or liquor.

We reached Southampton, as far as I remember, on a Saturday. On the boat I had worn a black suit, the white flannel one, which my friends had got me, having been kept especially for wearing when I landed. I had thought that white clothes would be the right thing when I stepped ashore, and therefore I did so in white flannels. Those were the last days of September, and I found I was the only person wearing such clothes. I left in charge of an agent all my kit, including the keys, seeing that many others also had done the same, and feeling I must follow suit.

I had four notes of introduction: to Dr P.J. Mehta, to Sjt. Dalpatram Shukla, to Prince Ranjitsinhji and to Dadabhai Naoroji, the Grand Old Man. Someone on board had advised us to put up at the Victoria Hotel in London. Sjt. Mazmudar and I accordingly went there. The embarrassment of being the only person in white clothes was already too much for me. And when at the hotel I was told that I would not get my things from the agent the next day, it being a Sunday, I was exasperated.

Dr Mehta, to whom I had wired from Southampton, called at about eight o'clock the same evening. He gave me a hearty greeting. He smiled at my being in flannels. As we were talking, I casually picked up his top-hat, and trying to see how smooth it was, passed my hand over it the wrong way and disturbed the fur. Dr Mehta looked somewhat angrily at what I was doing and stopped me. But the mischief was done. The incident was a warning for the future. This was my first lesson in European etiquette, into the details of which Dr Mehta gently initiated me. 'Do not touch other people's things,' he said. 'Do not ask questions as we usually do in India on first acquaintance; do not talk loudly; never address people as 'sir' whilst speaking to them as we do in India; only servants and subordinates address their masters that way.' And so on and so forth. He also told me that it was very expensive to live in a hotel and recommended that I should live with a private family. We deferred consideration of the matter until Monday.

Sjt. Mazmudar and I found the hotel to be a trying affair. It was also very expensive. There was, however, a Sindhi fellow-passenger from Malta who had become friends with Sjt. Mazmudar, and as he was not a stranger to London, he offered to find rooms for us. We agreed, and on Monday, as soon as we got our baggage, we paid up our bills and went to the rooms rented for us by the Sindhi friend. I remember my hotel bill came to over £3, an amount which shocked me. And I had practically starved in spite of this heavy bill! For I could relish nothing. Where I did not like one thing, I asked for another, but had to pay for both just the same. The fact is that all this while I had depended on the provisions which I had brought with me from Bombay.

I was very uneasy even in the new rooms. I would continually think of my home and country. My mother's love always haunted me. At night the tears would stream down my cheeks and home memories of all sorts made sleep out of the question. It was impossible to share my misery with anyone. And even if I could have done so, where was the use? I knew of nothing that would soothe me. Everything was strange—the people, their ways, and even their dwellings. I was a complete novice in the matter of English etiquette, and continually had to be on my guard. There was the additional inconvenience of the vegetarian vow. Even the dishes that I could eat, I then thought tasteless and insipid. I thus found myself between Scylla and Charybdis. England I could not bear, but to return to India was not to be thought of. Now that I had come, I must finish the three years, said the inner voice.

> Gandhiji had honed his 'Inner Voice' to such an extent that he actually heard it every time he took a major political decision. 'I believe that the inner voice is perfect knowledge or realization of the Truth ...'
>
> 'Definite rules have been laid down to help us realize truth, and we can know Truth only by following them. Hence, just as we cannot know geometry without studying it, so also it is not possible for anybody to hear the inner voice without necessary effort and training. Hence, according to my definition, a murderer cannot cite the inner voice in defence of his act.'
>
> (CWMG, Vol. 56, p. 182)

The Vow that Protected

D r Mehta went on Monday to the Victoria Hotel expecting to find me there. He discovered that we had left, got our new address, and met me at our rooms. He inspected my room and its appointments and shook his head in disapproval. 'This place won't do,' he said. 'We come to England not so much for the purpose of bookish studies as for gaining experience of English life and customs. And for this you need to live with a family. But before you do so, I think you had better serve a period of apprenticeship with—I will take you there.'

I gratefully accepted the suggestion and moved to the friend's room. He was all kindness and attention. He treated me as his own brother, initiated me into English ways and manners, and accustomed me to talking the language. My food, however, became a serious question. I could not relish boiled vegetables cooked without salt or condiments. The landlady did not know what to prepare for me. We had oatmeal porridge for breakfast which was fairly filling, but I always starved at lunch and dinner. The friend continually reasoned with me to eat meat, but I always pleaded my vow and then remained silent.

Day in and day out the friend would argue, but I had an eternal negative to face him with. The more he argued, the more uncompromising I became. Daily I would pray for God's protection and get it. Not that I had any idea of God. It was faith that was at work.

One day the friend began to read to me Bentham's *Theory of Utility*. I was at my wits' end. The language was too difficult for me to understand. He began to expound it. I said: 'Pray excuse me. These abstruse things are beyond me. I admit it may be necessary here to eat meat. But I cannot break my vow. I cannot argue about it. I am sure I cannot meet you in argument. But please give me up as foolish or obstinate. I appreciate your love for me and I know you to be my well-wisher. I also know that you are telling me again and again about this because you feel for me. But I am helpless. A vow is a vow. It cannot be broken.'

> 'It is my conviction that one cannot build one's character without the help of vows. They are to a man what an anchor is to a ship. A ship without an anchor is tossed to and fro and finally broken on the rocks; without vows, human beings meet a similar fate. The vow of truth includes all others.'
>
> (CWMG, Vol. 14, p. 97)

ॐ

> 'A vow can always be taken in regard to a good thing. There can never be a pledge to do an evil act. If anyone takes such a vow through ignorance, it becomes his duty to break it. For example, if a man takes a vow to act immorally, his awakening and his purification lie in his renouncing such a pledge. It is a sin to observe it.'
>
> (CWMG, Vol. 30, p. 313)

The friend looked at me in surprise. He closed the book and said: 'All right. I will not argue anymore.' I was glad. He never discussed the subject again. But he did not cease to worry about me. He smoked and drank, but he never asked me to do so. In fact he asked me to abstain from both. His one anxiety was that I might become very weak without meat, and thus be unable to feel at home in England.

That is how I served my apprenticeship for a month.

Affecting the English Gentleman

Meanwhile my friend had devised another way of winning me. His love for me led him to think, that if I persisted in my objections to meat-eating, I would not only develop a weak constitution, but would return to India as an ignorant man because I would never in my aloofness reap the benefit of the English stay.

But I decided that I should put him at ease, that I should assure him that I would be clumsy no more, but try to become polished and make up for my vegetarianism by cultivating other accomplishments which fitted one for polite society. And for this purpose I undertook the all too impossible task of becoming an English gentleman.

The clothes after the Bombay cut that I was wearing were, I thought, unsuitable for English society, and I got new ones at a fashionable tailor's. I also went in for a silk hat. Not content with this, I wasted ten pounds on an evening suit made in Bond Street; and got my good and noble-hearted brother to send me a double watch-chain of gold. It was not considered quite correct to wear a readymade tie and I learnt the art of tying one for myself. In India the mirror had been a luxury permitted on the days when the family barber gave me a shave. Here I wasted ten minutes every day before a large mirror watching myself arranging my tie and parting my hair in the correct fashion. My hair was by no means soft and every day it meant a regular struggle with the brush to keep it in position. Each time the hat was put on and off, the hand would automatically move towards the head to adjust the hair, not to mention the other civilised habit of the hand every now and then operating for the same purpose when sitting in polished society.

In 1917, Lord Irwin had criticized Gandhiji's manner of dressing. Gandhiji replied to the remarks of the Viceroy in a letter to The Pioneer:

'The fact is that I wear the national dress because it is the most natural and the most becoming for an Indian. I believe that our copying of the European dress is a sign of our degradation, humiliation and our weakness, and that we are committing a national sin in discarding a dress which is best suited to the Indian climate and which, for its simplicity, art and cheapness, is not to be beaten on the face of the earth and which answers hygienic requirements...

'I am sorry to inform Lord Irwin and your readers that my esteemed friend Babu Brijkishore Prasad, the Ex-hon. Member of council, still remains unregenerate and retains the provincial cap and never walks barefoot and "kicks up" a terrible noise even in the house we are living in by wearing wooden sandals. He has still not the courage, in spite of most admirable contact with me, to discard his semi-anglicized dress and whenever he goes to see officials puts his legs into the bifurcated garment and on his own admission tortures himself by cramping his feet in inelastic shoes. I cannot induce him to believe that his clients won't desert him and the courts won't punish him if he wore his more becoming and less expensive "dhoti".'

(CWMG, Vol. 13, pp. 450–1)

As if all this were not enough to make me look the thing, I directed my attention to other details that were supposed to go towards the making of an English gentleman. I had gathered that it would be the proper thing to take lessons in dancing, French and elocution. French was not only the language of neighbouring France, but it was the lingua franca of the Continent over which I had a desire to travel. I decided to take dancing lessons at a class and paid down £3 as fees for a term. I must have taken about six lessons in three weeks. But it was beyond me to achieve anything like rhythmic motion. I could not follow the piano and hence found it impossible to keep time. What then was I to do? The recluse in the fable kept a cat to keep off the rats, and then a cow to feed the cat with milk, and a man to keep the cow and so on. My ambitions also grew like the family of the

recluse. I thought I should learn to play the violin in order to cultivate an ear for Western music. So I invested £3 in a violin and something more in fees. I sought a third teacher to give me lessons in elocution and paid him a preliminary fee of a guinea. He recommended Bell's *Standard Elocutionist* as a textbook, which I purchased. And I began with a speech of Pitt's.

But Mr Bell rang the bell of alarm in my ear and I awoke.

I had not to spend a lifetime in England, I said to myself. What then was the use of learning elocution? And how could dancing make a gentleman of me? The violin I could learn even in India. I was a student and ought to go on with my studies. I should qualify myself for the Bar. If my character made a gentleman of me, so much the better. Otherwise I should forego the ambition.

These and similar thoughts possessed me, and I expressed them in a letter which I addressed to the elocution teacher, requesting him to excuse me from further lessons. I had taken only two or three. I wrote a similar letter to the dancing teacher, and went personally to the violin teacher with a request to dispose of the violin for any price it might fetch. She was friendly with me, so I told her how I had discovered that I was pursuing a false ideal. She encouraged me in the determination to make a complete change.

This infatuation must have lasted about three months. The punctiliousness in dress persisted for years. But henceforward I became a student.

A Shilling and Threepence a Day

Let no one imagine that my experiments in dancing and the like marked a stage of indulgence in my life. The reader will have noticed that there was a purpose behind the chase. The transition was therefore easy.

As I kept strict watch over my way of living, I could see that it was necessary to economize. I therefore decided to reduce my expenses by half. My accounts showed numerous items spent on fares. Again my living with a family meant the payment of a regular weekly bill.

So I decided to take rooms on my own account, instead of living any longer in a family and also to move from place to place according to the work I had to do, thus gaining experience at the same time. The rooms were so selected as to enable me to reach the place of business on foot in half an hour and so save fares. Before this I had always taken some kind of conveyance whenever I went anywhere, and had to find extra time for walks. The new arrangement combined walks and economy, as it meant a saving of fares and gave me walks of eight or ten miles a day. It was mainly this habit of long walks that kept me practically free from illness throughout my stay in England and gave me a fairly strong body.

Thus I rented a suite of rooms; one for a sitting-room and another for a bedroom. This was the second stage. The third was yet to come.

These changes saved me half the expense. But how was I to utilize the time? I knew that Bar examinations did not require much study, and I therefore did not feel pressed for time. My weak English was a perpetual worry to me. I should, I thought, not only be called to the Bar, but have some literary degree as well. I inquired about the Oxford and Cambridge University courses, consulted a few friends, and found that if I elected to go to either of these places, that would mean greater expense and a much longer stay in England than I was prepared for. A friend suggested that if I really wanted to have the satisfaction of taking a difficult examination, I should pass the London Matriculation. It meant a good deal of labour and much addition to my stock of general knowledge, without any extra expense worth the name. I welcomed the suggestion. But the syllabus frightened me. Latin and a modern language were compulsory! How was I to manage Latin? But the friend entered a strong plea for it: 'Latin is very valuable to lawyers. Knowledge of Latin is very useful in understanding law-books. And one paper in Roman law is entirely in Latin. Besides, knowledge of Latin means greater command over the English language.' The argument came home and I decided to learn Latin, no matter how difficult it might be. French I had already begun, so I thought that should be the modern language. I joined a private Matriculation class. Examinations were held every six months and I had only five months at my disposal. It was an almost impossible task for me. But the aspirant after being an English gentleman chose to convert himself into a serious student. I framed my own timetable to the minute; but neither my intelligence nor memory promised to enable me to tackle Latin and French besides other subjects within the given period. The result was that I failed in Latin. I was sorry but did not lose heart. I had acquired a taste for Latin, also I thought my French would be all the better for another trial and I would select a new subject in the science group. Chemistry which was my subject in science had no attraction for want of experiments. It was one of the compulsory subjects in India and so I had selected it for the London Matriculation. This time however I chose Heat and Light instead of Chemistry. It was said to be easy and I found it to be so.

With my preparation for another trial, I made an effort to simplify my life still further. I felt that my way of living did not yet become the modest means of my family. The thought of my struggling brother, who nobly responded to my regular calls for monetary help, deeply moved me. I saw that most of those who were spending from eight to fifteen pounds monthly had the advantage of scholarships. I had before me examples of much simpler living. I came across a fair number of poor students living more humbly than I. One of them was staying in slums in a room at two shillings a week and living on twopence worth of cocoa and bread for a meal from cheap Cocoa Rooms. It was far from me to think of emulating him, but I felt I could surely have one room instead of two and cook some of my meals at home. That would be a saving of four to five pounds each month. I also came across books on simple living. I gave up the suite of rooms and rented one instead, invested in a stove, and began cooking my breakfast at home. The process scarcely took me more than twenty minutes for there was only oatmeal porridge to cook and water to boil for cocoa. I had lunch out and for dinner had bread and cocoa at home. Thus I managed to live on a shilling and threepence a day. This was also a period of intensive study. Plain living saved me plenty of time and I passed my examination.

> *Gandhiji wrote to his son Harilal in a letter of 1918, encouraging him to do his own cooking when occasion demanded it:*
>
> *'It is true that cooking takes some time but I believe that this time is not wasted ... If I give my own example, when I was very busy with studies in England I did not take more than half an hour in the morning and in the evening for cooking. In the morning I used to prepare porridge and this took exactly twenty minutes; if I cooked in the evening, I prepared soup. As it did not require stirring, the only time spent was on getting materials ready. After putting the thing on the fire, I would sit and read ... This is only to illustrate that it is possible to do one's own cooking in a very short time.'*
>
> (CWMG, Vol. 15, p. 46)

৵

> *Self-cooking, indeed, helped one save money, in addition to one's learning an essential art. Gandhiji learnt his first lesson in thrift during this period.*
>
> *Appasaheb Patwardhan, Gandhiji's co-worker from 1919, describes it thus in an article written in commemoration of Gandhiji's seventy-fifth birthday:*
>
> *'Even before the war began, while paper was neither dear nor scarce, Bapu would never allow paper written only on one side to be thrown into the wastepaper basket. All such pastis were carefully sifted out from his voluminous incoming correspondence. He utilized the blank side for writing out drafts and other purposes. He cut up one notepaper into half a dozen tiny pieces and wrote out as many separate personal letters to the several ashramites dispatching them all in one cover.*
>
> *Indeed the Bapu, not only of the ashramites but of the famished millions of India, the votary of Daridranarayan, could ill afford to waste even a particle of food or a drop of water.'*

Let not the reader think that this living made my life by any means a dreary affair. On the contrary the change harmonized my inward and outward life. My life was now more truthful and my soul was full of joy.

Saved from Temptation

Alterations in my way of living led to changes in my diet. I studied vegetarianism, subscribed to a weekly, journal of the Vegetarian Society in England, joined the Society and soon found myself on its executive committee. I stopped taking sweets and condiments, also tea and coffee, and began to live largely on bread, cocoa and boiled vegetables. My experiments taught me that the real seat of taste is not the tongue but the mind.

I also made some acquaintance with various religions. Thanks to two Theosophist friends whom I met during the period, I was led to read the Bhagavad Gita for the first time. They invited me to read the *Song Celestial*— Sir Edwin Arnold's translation of the Gita—with them. I confessed with shame that though I had never read, either in the original or translation, what was regarded as our most sacred book, I should gladly read the English translation with them and help them in what humble way I could. So I began reading the Gita with them. The following verses in the second chapter made a deep impression on my mind and they still ring in my ears:

> If one
> Ponders on objects of the sense, there springs
> Attraction; from attraction grows desire,
> Desire flames to fierce passion, passion breeds

> Recklessness; then the memory—all betrayed—
> Lets noble purpose go, and saps the mind
> Till purpose, mind, and man are all undone.

The book struck me as one of priceless worth. It has afforded me invaluable help in my moments of gloom.

At the suggestion of a Christian friend from Manchester I read the Bible about the same time. Parts of the Old Testament through which I plodded with much difficulty, repelled me, but the New Testament, especially the Sermon on the Mount, captured me. I compared it with the Gita. The verses: 'But I say unto you, that ye resist not evil: but whosoever shall smite thee on thy right cheek, turn to him the other also,' delighted me beyond measure and I was reminded of the lines from the Gujarati poet Shamalbhatt quoted in a previous chapter: 'For a bowl of water, give a goodly meal'.

Though I had acquired a nodding acquaintance with Hinduism and other religions, I should have known that it would not be enough to save me in my trials.

During the last year of my stay in England I was invited with a friend to a Vegetarian Conference at Portsmouth. We were put up in a house about which the Reception Committee knew nothing, but which was a house of ill fame. After dinner we sat down to play whist, in which our landlady joined. Every player indulges in innocent jokes, but here my companion and the landlady began to make indecent ones as well. I was drawn into the temptation too, but just as I was about to go beyond the limit, leaving the cards and the game to themselves, God, through my good companion, uttered the blessed warning: 'Whence this devil in you, my boy! Be off, quick!'

I was ashamed. I took the warning and felt deeply grateful to the friend. I remembered the solemn vow I had taken before my mother, and fled from the scene.

I did not then know the essence of religion or of God, and how He works in us. Only vaguely I understood that God had saved me on that occasion. Indeed I rejoice to be able to say that on many occasions of trial He has saved me against myself. When every hope is gone, when 'helpers fail and comforts flee' I have known help to arrive somehow. Supplication, worship, prayer are no superstition; they are acts more real than the acts of eating, drinking, sitting or walking. It is no exaggeration to say that they alone are real, all else is unreal.

Back Home as Barrister

During this period my studies were not forgotten and at last, after nine months' intensive reading, I was called to the Bar on 10 June 1891. On the 12th I sailed for home, worried at my ignorance of Indian law and not at all confident of finding work. The passage from Aden was choppy. Almost every passenger was sick; I alone was in perfect form, staying on deck to see the stormy surge, and enjoying the splash of the waves. At breakfast, there would be just one or two people besides myself, eating their oatmeal porridge from plates carefully held in their laps, lest the porridge itself find its place there.

The outer storm was to me a symbol of the inner. But even as the former left me unperturbed, I think I can say the same thing about the latter.

My elder brother had come to meet me at the dock. The sad news was now given to me that my mother was no more. My brother had kept me ignorant of her death. He wanted to spare me the blow in a foreign land. The news, however, was none the less a severe shock to me. My grief was even greater than over my father's death. Most of my cherished hopes were shattered. But I remember that I did not give myself up to any wild expression of grief. I could even check the tears, and began life without any mourning interruption.

For a time I lived in Rajkot, but friends advised me to go to Bombay for some time in order to gain experience of the High Court, to study Indian law and to try and get what practice I could in Bombay. I took up the suggestion and went.

But it was impossible for me to get along in Bombay for more than four or five months, there being no income to square with the ever-increasing expenditure.

Disappointed, I left Bombay and went to Rajkot where I set up my own office. Here I got along moderately well. Drafting application and memorials brought me in, on an average, Rs 300 a month. For this work I had to thank influence rather than my own ability, for my brother's partner had a settled practice. All applications, etc., which were, really or to his mind, of an important character, he sent to big barristers. To my lot fell the applications to be drafted on behalf of his poor clients.

I Go to South Africa

But soon I became choked with the intriguing atmosphere of Kathiawad, and when a Memon firm from Porbander offered me work in South Africa, I readily accepted the offer. There was an important lawsuit concerning a claim for £40,000 which the firm of Dada Abdulla & Co. were making against their rivals Taib Haji Khanmamad. A partner in the former firm offered me first class return fare, all expenses and £105 if I would go to work for them in South Africa for a year. So I left India for South Africa in April 1893.

The port of Natal is Durban. Abdulla Sheth was there to receive me. As the ship arrived at the quay, and I watched the people coming on board to meet their friends, I observed that the Indians were held in scant respect by Europeans. I could not fail to notice a sort of superiority about the manner in which those who knew Abdulla Sheth behaved towards him, and it stung me. Abdulla Sheth had got used to it. Those who looked at me did so with a certain amount of curiosity. My dress marked me out from other Indians. I had a frock-coat and a turban, an imitation of the Bengal *pugree*.

I was taken to the firm's quarters and shown into the room set apart for me, next to Abdulla Sheth's. He did not then understand me, I could not understand him. He read the papers his brother had sent through me, and felt more puzzled. He thought his brother had sent him a white elephant. My style of dress and living struck him as being expensive like that of the Europeans. There was no particular work then which could be given to me. Their case was going on in the Transvaal. There was no meaning in sending me there immediately. And how far could he trust my ability and honesty? He would not be in Pretoria to watch me. The defendants were in Pretoria, and for aught he knew, they might win me over to their side. And if work in connection with the case in question was not to be entrusted to me, what work could I be given to do, as all other work could be done much better by his clerks? The clerks could be brought to book, if they did wrong. Could I be treated similarly, if I also happened to err? So if no work in connection with the case could be given to me, I should have to be kept for nothing.

Abdulla Sheth was practically unlettered, but he had a rich fund of experience. He had an acute intellect and was conscious of it. By practice he had picked up just sufficient English for conversational purposes, but that served him for carrying on all his business, whether it was dealing with Bank Managers and European merchants or explaining his case to his counsel. The Indians held him in very high esteem. His firm was then the biggest, or at any rate one of the biggest Indian firms.

On the second or third day of my arrival, he took me to see the Durban Court. There he introduced me to several people and seated me next to his attorney. The Magistrate kept staring at me and finally asked me to take off my turban, which I refused to do, and left the court.

So here too there was fighting in store for me.

Abdulla Sheth explained to me why some Indians were required to take off their turbans. Those wearing the Mussalman costume might, he said, keep their turbans on, but the other Indians on entering a court had to take theirs off as a rule.

Removing one's turban would be pocketing an insult. So I thought I had better bid goodbye to the Indian turban and begin wearing an English hat, which would save me from the insult and the unpleasant controversy.

But Abdulla Sheth disapproved of the idea. He said, 'If you do anything of the kind it will have a very bad effect. You will compromise those insisting on wearing Indian turbans. And an Indian turban sits well on your head. If you wear an English hat you will pass for a waiter.'

There was practical wisdom, patriotism, and a little bit of narrowness in this advice.

On the whole I liked Abdulla Sheth's advice. I wrote to the press about the incident and defended the wearing of my turban in the court. The question was very much discussed in the papers, which described me as an 'unwelcome visitor'. Thus the incident gave me an unexpected advertisement in South Africa within a few days of my arrival there. Some supported me, while others severely criticized my temerity.

Abdulla Sheth did not have to wait long before finding work for me. My presence was necessary in Pretoria for his case. On the seventh or eighth day after my arrival, I left Durban. A first class seat was booked for me. It was usual there to pay five shillings extra, if one needed bedding. Abdulla Sheth insisted that I should book one bedding but out of obstinacy and pride, and with a view to saving five shillings, I declined. Abdulla Sheth warned me. 'Look, now,' said he, 'this is a different country from India. Thank God, we have enough and to spare. Please do not stint yourself in anything that you may need.'

I thanked him and asked him not to be anxious.

The train reached Maritzburg, the capital of Natal, at about 9 p.m. Beddings used to be provided at this station. A railway servant came and asked me if I wanted one. 'No,' said I, 'I have one with me.' He went away. But a passenger came next, and looked me up and down. He saw that I was a 'coloured' man. This disturbed him. Out he went and came in again with one or two officials. They all kept quiet, when another official came to me and said, 'Come along, you must go to the van compartment.'

'But I have a first class ticket,' said I.

'That doesn't matter,' rejoined the other. 'I tell you, you must go to the van compartment.'

'I tell you, I was permitted to travel in this compartment at Durban, and I insist on going on in it.'

'No, you won't,' said the official. 'You must leave this compartment, or else I shall have to call a police constable to pull you out.'

'Yes, you may. I refuse to get out voluntarily.'

The constable came. He took me by the hand and pushed me out. My luggage was also taken out. I refused to go to the other compartment and the train steamed away. I went and sat in the waiting room, keeping my handbag with me, and leaving the other luggage where it was. The railway authorities had taken charge of it.

It was winter, and winter in the higher regions of South Africa is severely cold. Maritzburg being at a high altitude, the cold was bitter. My overcoat was in my luggage, but I did not dare to ask for it lest I might be insulted again, so I sat and shivered. There was no light in the room. A passenger came in at about midnight and possibly wanted to talk to me. But I was in no mood to talk.

I began to think of my duty. Should I fight for my rights or go back to India, or should I go on to Pretoria without minding the insults, and return to India after finishing the case? It would be cowardice to run back to India without fulfilling my obligation. The hardship to which I was subjected, was superficial—only a symptom of the deep disease of colour prejudice. I should try, if possible, to root out the disease and suffer hardships in the process. Redress for personal wrongs I should seek only to the extent that would be necessary for the removal of the colour prejudice.

So I decided at any cost to take the next available train to Pretoria.

The following morning I sent a long telegram to the General Manager of the railway, and also informed Abdulla Sheth, who immediately met the General Manager. The Manager justified the conduct of the railway authorities, but informed him that he had already instructed the Station Master to see that I boarded the train safely. Abdulla Sheth had also wired to the Indian merchants in Maritzburg and to friends in other places to meet me and look after me. The merchants came to see me at the station and tried to comfort me by narrating their own hardships and explaining that what had happened to me was nothing unusual. They also said that Indians travelling first or second class had to expect trouble from railway officials and white passengers. The day was thus spent in listening to these tales of woe. The evening train arrived. There was a reserved berth for me. I now purchased at Maritzburg the bedding ticket I had refused to book at Durban.

The train took me to Charlestown, and from there I continued my journey, not without hardship, by coach to Johannesburg and thence by train to Pretoria.

Servant of the Community

Thus in 1893, I was in full possession of facts about the Indian position in South Africa. But I did nothing tangible beyond occasionally talking with the Indians in Pretoria on the subject. It appeared to me that to look after the firm's case and to take up the question of the Indian grievances in South Africa at the same time was not feasible. I could see that trying to do both would be to damage both. The year 1894 was thus already upon me. The case that had brought me to South Africa was satisfactorily settled, and so I returned to Durban and prepared to return to India. At the farewell entertainment held by Dada Abdulla, someone put a copy of the *Natal Mercury* in my hands. I read it and found that the detailed report of the proceedings of the Natal Legislative Assembly contained a few lines under the caption 'Indian Franchise'. The Natal Government was about to introduce a Bill to disfranchise Indians, which could only be the beginning of the end of what little rights they were then enjoying. I suspended my departure for India. The same night I drew up a petition to be presented to the Legislative Assembly. A telegram was sent to the Government requesting a delay of proceedings. A committee was appointed at once with Sheth Abdulla as chairman and the telegram was sent in his name. The further reading of the Bill was postponed for two days. That petition was the first ever sent by the Indians to a South African legislature. It did create an impression although it failed to defeat the Bill. This was the South African Indians' first experience of such an agitation, and a new thrill of enthusiasm passed through the community. Meetings were held every day, and more and more persons attended them. The requisite funds were oversubscribed. Many volunteers helped in preparing copies, securing signatures and similar work without any remuneration. There were others who both worked and subscribed to the funds. The descendants of ex-indentured Indians joined the movement with alacrity. They knew English and wrote a fine hand. They did copying and other work ungrudgingly day and night. Within a month a memorial with ten thousand signatures was forwarded to Lord Ripon, who was then Colonial Secretary, and the immediate task I had set before myself was done.

I therefore asked for leave to return home. But the agitation had aroused such keen interest among the Indians that they would not let me go. They said: 'You yourself have explained to us that this is the first step taken with a view to our ultimate extinction. Who knows whether the Colonial Secretary will return a favourable reply to our memorial? You have witnessed our enthusiasm. We are willing and ready to work and pay. But for want of a guide, what little has been done will go for nothing. We therefore think it is your duty to stay on'. I felt the force of the argument and saw that it would be well if a permanent organization was formed to watch Indian interests. So again I stayed. The Natal Indian Congress was duly organized, and God laid the foundation of my life in South Africa and sowed the seed of the fight for national self-respect. The Congress was founded about May 1894.

I am compelled to omit the remarkable subsequent history of the Congress, how it was confronted with difficulties, how Government officials attacked it and how it escaped scatheless from those attacks. But one fact must be placed on record. Steps were taken to save the community from the habit of exaggeration. Attempts were always made to draw their attention to their own shortcomings. Whatever force there was in the arguments of the Europeans was duly acknowledged. Every occasion, when it was possible to cooperate with the Europeans on terms of equality and consistent with self-respect, was heartily taken. The newspapers were supplied with as much information about the Indian movement as they would publish, and whenever Indians were unfairly attacked in the Press replies were sent to the newspapers concerned.

Rumblings of the Storm

By now I had been three years in South Africa. I had got to know the people and they had got to know me. I had established a fairly good practice and could see that people felt the need of my presence. I, therefore, made up my mind to go back home to fetch my wife and children and then return and settle there. So in 1896, I went to India for six months with the leave of the community. I had hardly completed that period in India, when I received a cablegram from Natal asking me to return at once, and so I did. Dada Abdulla had just then purchased the steamship *Courland* and he insisted on my travelling in that boat, offering to take me and my family free of charge. I gratefully accepted the offer and in the beginning of December I set sail from Bombay a second time for Natal, now with my wife and two sons. Another steamship *Naderi* also sailed for Durban at the same time. The total number of passengers these boats carried must have been about eight hundred, half of whom were bound for the Transvaal.

Since the steamer was making straight for Natal, without calling at intermediate ports, our voyage was only eighteen days. But as though to warn us of the coming real storm on land a terrible

gale overtook us, whilst we were only four days from Natal. December is a
summer month of monsoon in the southern hemisphere, and so gales, great
and small, are quite common in the southern seas at that season. The gale
in which we were caught was so violent and prolonged, that the passengers
became alarmed. It was a solemn scene. All became one in face of the
common danger. They forgot their differences, and began to think of the one
and only God—Mussalmans, Hindus, Christians and all. Some took various
vows. The captain also joined the passengers in their prayers. He assured them
all that though the storm was not without danger, he had had experience of
many worse ones, and explained to them that a well-built ship could stand
almost any weather. But they were inconsolable. Every minute were heard
sounds and crashes which foreboded breaches and leaks. The ship rocked and
rolled to such an extent that it seemed as though she would capsize at any
moment. It was out of the question for anyone to remain on deck. 'His will
be done!' was the one cry on every lip. So far as I can recollect we must have
been in this plight for about twenty-four hours. At last the sky cleared, the
sun made an appearance, and the captain said that the storm had blown over.
People's faces beamed with gladness, and with the disappearance of danger
disappeared also the name of God from their lips. Eating and drinking, singing
and merrymaking again became the order of the day. The fear of death was
gone, and the momentary mood of earnest prayer gave place to *maya*.

> *The famous word in Hindu philosophy is nearly untranslatable, but has been frequently
> translated in English as 'delusion', 'illusion'. Gandhiji wrote in a letter, 'I believe in the
> theory of maya in my own way. In the cycle of Time this universe is maya, but during the
> moment of time it exists, it is real enough.'*

> *(CWMG, Vol. 51, p. 40)*

ॐ

> *In another letter on the subject of maya, he wrote: 'As a matter of fact, it is a creation of
> our imagination even as the snake in the rope is. The real universe, like the real rope, is
> there. We perceive ... when the veil is lifted and [the] darkness is gone ...'*

> *(CWMG, Vol. 45, p. 52)*

There were of course the usual *namaz* and the prayers, but they had none of the solemnity of that dread hour.

The storm had made me one with the passengers. I had little fear of the storm, for I had had experience of similar ones. I am a good sailor and do not get sea-sick. So I could fearlessly move amongst the passengers bringing them comfort and good cheer, and conveying to them hourly reports from the captain. The friendship I thus formed stood me, as we shall see, in very good stead.

The ship cast anchor in the port of Durban on the 18th or 19th of December. The *Naderi* also arrived the same day. The real storm was now on.

Lynched

After twenty-three days' political quarantine in the bay, the ships
were brought into the dock and the passengers began to go ashore.
But Mr Escombe, a member of the Government, had sent word to the
captain that as the whites were highly enraged against me, and my life
was in danger, I and my family should be advised to land at dusk, when
the Port Superintendent, Mr Tatum, would escort us home. The captain
communicated the message to me, and I agreed to act accordingly. But
scarcely half an hour after this Mr Laughton, a well-known advocate, came
on board and said to the captain: 'I would like to take Mr Gandhi with me,
should he have no objection. As the legal adviser of the Agent Company
I tell you that you are not bound to carry out the message you have
received from Mr Escombe.' After this he came to me, and said somewhat
to this effect: 'If you are not afraid, I suggest that Mrs Gandhi and the
children should drive to Mr Rustomji's house, whilst you and I walk out
the distance. I do not at all like the idea of your entering the city like a
thief in the night. I do not think there is any fear of anyone hurting you.
Everything is quiet now. The whites have all dispersed. But in any case
I am convinced that you ought not to enter the city stealthily.' I readily
agreed. My wife and children drove safely to Mr Rustomji's place. With

the captain's permission I went ashore with Mr Laughton. Mr Rustomji's house was about two miles from the dock.

As soon as we landed, some European youngsters recognized me and shouted, 'Gandhi! Gandhi!' About half a dozen men rushed to the spot, and joined in the shouting. Mr Laughton feared that the crowd might swell, and he hailed a rickshaw. I had never liked the idea of being in a rickshaw. This was to be my first experience. But the youngsters would not let me get into it. They frightened the rickshaw boy out of his life, and he took to his heels. As we walked on, the crowd continued to swell, until it became impossible to proceed further. They first caught hold of Mr Laughton, and separated him from me. Then they pelted me with stones, brickbats and rotten eggs.

Someone snatched away my turban, whilst others began to batter and kick me. I fainted and caught hold of the front railings of a house, and stood there to get my breath. But it was impossible. They came upon me boxing and battering. The wife of the Police Superintendent, who knew me, happened to be passing by. The brave lady came up, opened her parasol though there was no sun then, and stood between the crowd and me. This checked the fury of the mob, as it was difficult for them to deliver blows on me without harming Mrs Alexander.

Meanwhile an Indian youth who had witnessed the incident had run to the police station. The Police Superintendent Mr Alexander sent a posse of men to escort me safely to my destination. They arrived in time. The police station lay on our way. When we reached it, the Superintendent asked me to take refuge in the station, but I gratefully declined the offer. 'They are sure to quiet down when they realize their mistake,' I said: 'I have trust in their sense of fairness'. Escorted by the police I arrived without further harm at Mr Rustomji's house. I had bruises all over, but no abrasions except in one place. Dr Dadibarjor, the ship's doctor, who was on the spot, rendered the best possible help.

There was quiet inside, but outside the whites surrounded the house. Night was coming on, and the yelling crowd was shouting, 'We must have Gandhi!' The quick-sighted Police Superintendent was already there trying to keep the crowds under control, not by threats but by humouring them. But he was not entirely free from anxiety. He sent me a message to this effect: 'If you would save your friend's house and property and also your family, you should escape from the house in disguise, as I suggest.'

As suggested by the Superintendent, I put on an Indian constable's uniform and wore on my head a deep, metal basin hidden under a Madras turban. Two detectives accompanied me, one of them disguised as an Indian merchant, his face painted to resemble that of an Indian. I forget the disguise of the other. We reached a neighbouring shop through a bylane, and making our way through the gunny bags piled in the godown, escaped by the gate of the shop, and threaded our way through the crowd to a carriage that had been kept ready at the end of the street. In this we drove off to the same police station where Mr Alexander had offered me refuge a short time before, and I thanked him and the detective officers.

Whilst I had been thus effecting my escape, Mr Alexander had kept the crowd amused by singing the tune:

> 'Hang old Gandhi
> On the sour apple tree.'

When he was informed of my safe arrival at the police station, he thus broke the news to the crowd: 'Well, your victim has made good his escape through the adjoining shop. You had better go home now'. Some of them were angry, others laughed, some refused to believe the story.

'Well then', said the Superintendent, 'if you do not believe me, you may appoint one or two representatives, whom I am ready to take inside the house. If they succeed in finding out Gandhi, I will gladly deliver him to you. But if they fail, you must disperse. I am sure that you have no intention of destroying Mr Rustomji's house or of harming Mr Gandhi's wife and children.'

The crowd sent their representatives to search the house. They soon returned with disappointing news, and the crowd broke up at last, most of them admiring the Superintendent's tactful handling of the situation, and a few fretting and fuming.

The late Mr Chamberlain, who was then Secretary of State for the Colonies, cabled asking the Natal Government to prosecute my assailants. Mr Escombe sent for me, expressed his regret for the injuries I had sustained and said: 'Believe me, I cannot feel happy over the least little injury done to your person. You had a right to accept Mr Laughton's advice, and to face the worst, but I am sure that if you had considered my suggestion favourably, these sad occurrences would not have happened. If you can identify the assailants, I am prepared to arrest and prosecute them. Mr Chamberlain also desires me to do so.'

To which I gave the following reply:

'I do not want to prosecute anyone. It is possible that I might be able to identify one or two of them, but what is the use of getting them punished? Besides I do not hold the assailants to blame. They were given to understand that I had made exaggerated statements in India about the whites in Natal, and calumniated them. If they believed these reports, it is no wonder that they were enraged. The leaders, and, if you will permit me to say so, you are to blame. You could have guided the people properly, but you also believed Reuter, and assumed that I must have indulged in exaggeration. I do not want to bring anyone to book. I am sure that when the truth becomes known, they will be sorry for their conduct.'

'Would you mind giving me this in writing?' said Mr Escombe. 'Because I shall have to cable to Mr Chamberlain to that effect. I do not want you to make any statement in haste. You may, if you like, consult Mr Laughton and your other friends, before you come to a final decision. I may confess, however, that if you waive the right of bringing your assailants to book, you will considerably help me in restoring quiet, besides enhancing your own reputation.'

'Thank you,' said I. 'I need not consult anyone. I had made my decision in the matter before I came to you. It is my conviction that I should not prosecute the assailants and I am prepared this moment to reduce my decision to writing.'

With this I gave him the necessary statement.

I had not yet left the police station when, after two days, I was taken to see Mr Escombe. Two constables were sent to protect me, though no such precaution was then needed.

On the day of landing, as soon as the yellow flag was lowered, a
representative of the *Natal Advertiser* had come to interview me. He had
asked me a number of questions, and in reply I had been able to refute
every one of the charges that had been levelled against me. Thanks to Sir
Phirozeshah Mehta, I had delivered only written speeches in India, and
I had copies of them all, as well as of my other writings. I had given the
interviewer all this literature, and showed him that in India I had said nothing
which I had not already said in South Africa in stronger language. I had also
shown him that I had had no hand in bringing the passengers of the *Courland*
and *Naderi* to South Africa. Many of them were old residents, and most of
them, far from wanting to stay in Natal, meant to go to the Transvaal. In
those days the Transvaal offered better prospects than Natal to those coming
in search of wealth, and most Indians, therefore, preferred to go there.

This interview and my refusal to prosecute the assailants produced such a
profound impression that the Europeans of Durban were ashamed of their
conduct. The press declared me to be innocent and condemned the mob.
Thus the lynching ultimately proved to be a blessing for me, that is, for the
cause. It enhanced the prestige of the Indian community in South Africa,
made my work easier, and the experience prepared me for the practice
of Satyagraha.

In three or four days, I went to my house and it was not long before I settled
down again.

My Own Dhobi

I had started on a life of ease and comfort but the experiment was short-lived. Although I had furnished the house with care, it failed to have any hold on me. So no sooner had I launched forth on that life, than I began to cut down expenses. The washerman's bill was heavy and as also he was by no means noted for his punctuality, even two to three dozen shirts and collars proved insufficient for me. Collars had to be changed daily and shirts, if not daily, at least every alternate day. This meant a double expense, which appeared to me unnecessary. So I equipped myself with a washing outfit to save it. I bought a book on washing, studied the art and taught it also to my wife. This no doubt added to my work, but its novelty made it a pleasure.

I shall never forget the first collar that I starched. I had used more starch than necessary, the iron had not been made hot enough and for fear of burning the collar I had not pressed it sufficiently. The result was that, though the collar was fairly stiff, the superfluous starch continually dusted the jacket. I went to court with the collar on, thus inviting the ridicule of brother barristers, but even in those days I could be impervious to ridicule.

'Well,' said I, 'this is my first experiment in washing my own collars, and hence the loose starch. But it does not trouble me and then there is the advantage of providing you with so much fun.'

'But surely there is no lack of laundries here?' asked a friend.

'The laundry bill is very heavy,' said I. 'The charge for washing a collar is almost as much as its price, and even then there is the eternal dependence on the washerman. I prefer by far to wash my things myself.'

But I could not make my friends appreciate the beauty of self-help. In course of time I became an expert washerman so far as my own work went, and my washing was by no means inferior to laundry washing. My collars were no less stiff or shiny than others.

A Recollection and Penance

Whether in Durban or in Johannesburg I had friends living with me and sometimes office clerks, all of whom became members of the family. I may indeed claim that I have known no distinction between relatives and strangers, countrymen and foreigners, white and coloured. It is no special virtue, it is part of my nature. When I was practising in Durban a number of office clerks were thus members of the household. One of these was a Christian, born of so-called 'untouchable' parents. Much of the work in the house, including cleaning chamber-pots, would be done by the members of this big family, but as the Christian clerk was a newcomer, it was our duty to attend to his bedroom. My wife, when the work fell to her lot, would readily attend to the needs of the others, but she had not conquered her prejudice against the 'untouchables'. Not without reluctance did she attend to this newcomer's room, and once I could not help noticing the frown on her face as, chamber-pot in hand, she was descending the staircase. I was a cruelly kind husband and was therefore not satisfied by her doing this duty with so much reluctance. I thought I must impose my will on her and make her do the thing cheerfully! My anger prevented me from seeing that compulsion and cheerfulness go ill together, and I shouted: 'I will not stand this nonsense in *my* house.'

'Keep your house to yourself then and let me go,' she sharply shouted back. I forgot myself, caught her by the hand, dragged her to the door and proceeded to open it with a view to pushing her out. The tears were rushing down her cheeks and she cried: 'Have you lost all sense of shame? Must you so far forget yourself? Where am I to go? I have no one here to go to. You think I must put up with your cuffs and kicks because I am your wife. For Heaven's sake behave yourself, and shut the door. Let us not be found making scenes like this!'

I put on a brave face, but was really ashamed. If my wife could not leave me, neither could I leave her. We have had many a tiff like this, but the end has always been peace and deeper understanding. The wife, with her matchless powers of endurance, has always got the better of me. I am no longer a blind, infatuated husband, no more presuming to be her teacher. We are tried friends, the one no longer regarding the other as an object of lust. She has been a faithful nurse throughout my illnesses, serving without any thought of receiving even so much as thanks, and in utter self-effacement she has followed me in all the important steps I have taken.

In a tribute to Kasturba who died in 1944, Gandhiji said to a relative:

'Ba was in no way weaker than I; in fact she was stronger. If I had not had her cooperation I would have been sunk. It was that illiterate woman who helped me to observe all my vows with the utmost strictness and kept me ever vigilant. Similarly, in politics also, she displayed great courage and took part in all the campaigns. From the worldly point of view, she may have been illiterate, but she was an ideal woman who had received what I regard as true education. She was a devout Vaishnava, used to worship the tulsi, religiously observed sacred days and continued to wear the necklace of holy beads right up to her death. I have given that necklace to this girl. But she loved the Harijan girl as much as she loved Manu or Devdas's Tara. She was the living image of the virtues of a Vaishnava described by Narasinha

Mehta in his bhajan. It is because of her that I am today what I am. She never spared herself, no matter how ill she herself was, in serving me. And often I have been in danger of my life. In the fast of 1943, I may say I was nearly at death's door, but she never cried or lost courage but on the contrary, kept up other people's courage and prayed to God. I can see her vivid face even today.'

(CWMG, Vol. 88, pp. 105–6)

Boer War Experiences

I must skip many other experiences of the period
between 1897 and 1899 and come straight to
the Boer War.

When the war was declared, my personal
sympathies were all with the Boers, but I
believed then that I had yet no right, in such
cases, to enforce my individual convictions. I have
minutely dealt with the inner struggle regarding
this in my *History of Satyagraha in South Africa,* and
I invite the curious to turn to those pages. Suffice
it to say, that my loyalty to the British rule drove
me to participation with the British in that war. I
felt, that if I demanded rights as a British citizen,
it was also my duty, as such, to participate in
the defence of the British Empire. I held then, that
India could achieve her complete emancipation
only within and through the British Empire. So I
collected together as many comrades as possible,

and with very great difficulty got their services accepted as an ambulance corps.

The average Englishman believed that the Indian was a coward, incapable of taking risks or looking beyond his immediate self-interest. Many English friends, therefore, threw cold water on my plan. But Dr Booth, of the Indian Church Mission, supported it wholeheartedly. He trained us in ambulance work. We secured medical certificates of fitness for service, and applied at last for service at the front.

Our corps was 1,100-strong, with nearly forty leaders. About 300 were free Indians, and the rest indentured. Dr Booth was also with us. The corps acquitted itself well. Though our work was to be outside the firing line, and though we had the protection of the Red Cross, we were asked at a critical moment to serve within the firing line. The reservation had not been of our seeking. The authorities did not want us to be within the range of fire. The situation however was changed after the reverse at Spion Kop, and General Buller sent the message that, though we were not bound to take the risk, the Government would be thankful if we would take it, and fetch the wounded from the field. We had no hesitation, and so the action at Spion Kop found us working within the firing line. On this occasion we had to march from twenty to twenty-five miles a day, bearing the wounded on stretchers. Amongst the wounded we had the honour of carrying soldiers like General Woodgate.

The corps was disbanded after six weeks' service, but our humble work was, at the moment, much applauded, and the Indians' prestige was enhanced. The newspapers published laudatory rhymes with the refrain, 'We are sons of Empire after all'.

I cannot forbear from recording a sweet reminiscence of how human nature shows itself at its best in moments of trial. We were marching towards Chievely Camp near Colenso where Lieutenant Roberts, the son of Lord Roberts, had received a mortal wound. Our corps had the honour of carrying the body from the field. It was a sultry day, the day of our march. Everyone was thirsting for water. There was a tiny brook on the way where we could slake our thirst. But who was to drink first? We had proposed to come in after the tommies had finished. But they would not begin first, and urged us to do so, and for a while a pleasant competition went on for giving precedence to one another.

Before closing this chapter, I must place a noteworthy incident on record. Among those who were in Ladysmith when it was invaded by the Boers, there were, besides Englishmen, a few stray Indian settlers. Some of these were traders, while the rest were indentured labourers working on the railways or as servants to Europeans. One of these was Parbhusingh. The officer in command at Ladysmith assigned various duties to every resident of the place. Perhaps the most dangerous and most responsible work was assigned to Parbhusingh, who was a 'coolie'. On a hill near Ladysmith the Boers had planted their pom-pom, whose operations destroyed many buildings and even occasioned some loss of life. An interval of a minute or two must pass before a shell which had been fired from such a gun reached a distant objective. If the besieged got some previous notice, they could take cover before the shell dropped in their midst. Parbhusingh used to sit perched up in a tree, all the time that the gun was working, with his eyes fixed on the hill, and he rang a bell the moment he observed the flash. On hearing the bell, the residents of Ladysmith instantly took cover and saved themselves from the deadly cannon ball whose approach was thus announced.

The story of his bravery at last reached the ears of Lord Curzon, then Viceroy of India, who sent a Kashmir robe for presentation to Parbhusingh.

To India and Back

On my return from War duty I felt that my work was now more in
India than South Africa, and I requested my co-workers to relieve
me. They accepted my request on condition that I should be ready to go
back to South Africa, if, within a year, the community should need me. The
warmth of farewell was overwhelming. The gifts included things in gold and
silver and even diamonds. Whilst they filled me with gratitude, they served
as an object lesson in trusteeship. I passed a sleepless night over them and
decided that I must hand them back to the community to be held in trust for
its service. The decision was given effect to, not without much
heartburn on the part of my wife then; but the years that have gone by
have convinced her also of the wisdom of the step. The conviction has ever
grown on me that a public worker should accept no gifts.

When I reached home the Congress which was held that year
in Calcutta, afforded me considerable opportunity for service.
I gave the volunteers some object lessons in sweeping and scavenging,
and had the honour of working as clerk and bearer to Sjt. Ghoshal who
was one of the general secretaries. I also had the privilege of moving a
resolution on the situation in South Africa, thanks to the good offices of
Gokhale, who ever since my arrival in India had treated me as a younger

brother. He took a keen interest in all my activities and introduced me to all the important people whom he thought I should know. To see him at work was as much a joy as an education. Whatever he did had reference only to the good of the country. He was very anxious that I should settle down in Bombay, practise at the Bar and help him in public work, which meant Congress work. I liked his advice but was diffident of success as a barrister.

I started work at Rajkot and was doing very well, when my friend and well-wisher, Sjt. Kevalram Dave who was mainly responsible for sending me to England, urged me to settle in Bombay. Here too I prospered better than I had expected. My South African clients often entrusted me with work and it was enough to enable me to pay my way. But just when I seemed to be settling down, I received an urgent cable summoning me to reach South Africa. Conformably to my promise I started at once.

I will not take the reader through the painful details of the political situation I found in South Africa. The War, and with it the services rendered by the Indians, were forgotten. The plight of the Indian settlers had gone from bad to worse and fresh disabilities were being heaped on them. I saw that I was now in for a long and indefinite stay in South Africa, if I was to serve my countrymen there. I decided to set up office in Johannesburg and with some difficulty succeeded in securing rooms in the legal quarters of the city.

With the determination to devote myself wholly to the cause of the community came increasing introspection stimulated by a fresh reading of the Gita.

This time too it was with a few theosophists that I had to read the Gita, and I did so with much more penetration than before. I even tried to memorize the verses and remember having learnt by heart no less than thirteen chapters. The Gita now became for me an infallible guide of conduct. It became my dictionary of reference. The words like *a-parigraha* (non-possession) and *samabhava* (equability) gripped me. How to divest oneself of all possessions, how to cultivate and preserve equability, became an absorbing question for me. Was I to burn my boats, give up all and follow Him? Straight came the answer: I could not follow Him unless I gave up all I had. It became clear as daylight to me that non-possession and equability presupposed a change of heart, a change of attitude. I wrote to Bombay advising my friends to allow my insurance policy to lapse, and wrote to my brother saying that although I had placed at his disposal all that I had saved up to that moment, henceforth he should expect nothing from me, for all future savings if any would be utilized for the benefit of the community.

About this time also (1904) I accepted responsibility for editing a weekly called *Indian Opinion,* dealing with the problems affecting the welfare of the Indians in South Africa. I soon discovered that it could not go on without my financial help. I kept on pouring out my savings until ultimately I was practically sinking all of them in it. *Indian Opinion* in those days, like *Young India* and *Navajivan* today, was a mirror of my life. I cannot recall a word in those articles set down without deliberation, or anything written in exaggeration or malice. Indeed the journal became for me training in self-restraint and I know that its tone compelled the critic to put a curb on his own pen. It was in the columns of this journal that I wrote a series of articles on dietetics which were later on published in book form and translated into English in the form of a book called *Guide to Health* which seems to have profoundly influenced the lives of many readers in the East and the West.

> *In* Guide to Health, *published in 1913 as* General Knowledge about Health *in English, Gandhiji wrote:*
>
> *'Tea, coffee, cocoa, all have a certain property that weakens our digestive powers. They are intoxicants because they form a habit which cannot be broken. When the author was in the habit of drinking tea, he felt lethargic if he did not get tea at the usual hour—this is the conclusive test of an intoxicant...'*
>
> *'As regards coffee, there is a couplet which has become well known:*
> *"Counters phlegm and wind, but lowers vigour and strength*
> *And turns blood to water—merits against three faults."'*
>
> *'... Coffee may have the virtue of counteracting phlegm and wind. But so have some other substances. Those who wish to drink coffee for the first two reasons should take a little ginger juice...'*

☙

About cocoa he wrote:

'*Cocoa has not yet become so popular because it is slightly more expensive than tea. Fortunately for us, we have not yet made friends with it, but it holds strong enough sway in fashionable homes.*'

'*Cocoa shares the defects of coffee. Like tea, it also contains a substance which has the effect of making the skin rough.*'

(CWMG, Vol.11, pp. 482–3)

ॐ

The book General Knowledge about Health *was revised by Gandhiji in 1942, during his imprisonment, as* Key to Health. *In his Preface to it, Gandhi wrote:*

'*...the book became the most popular of all my writings. I have never been able to understand the reason for this popularity. I had written those articles casually, and I did not attach much importance to them. But perhaps the reason for the popularity is to be sought in the fact that I have looked upon the problem of health from a novel point of view, somewhat different from orthodox methods adopted by doctors and vaidyas.... There is no fundamental difference between my ideas of today and those of 1906. But my mind is responsive. Therefore, whatever change the reader may find will, I hope, be in the nature of a progress.*'

(CWMG, Vol.76, pp. 411–12)

The Magic Spell of a Book

The influence of certain books on my life has indeed been very great, but no book has worked such a revolutionary change in my life as Ruskin's *Unto This Last*. In 1904 I had to go to Durban to put the affairs of *Indian Opinion* in order. Mr Albert West, an English friend, who was a practical printer and who had left his business at a moment's notice from me, had gone at my request to Durban to overhaul the transactions in connection with *Indian Opinion,* and had reported that the financial position of the paper was in a bad way.

As I was going to the station to catch the Durban train, Mr Polak who had by that time come into my life gave me *Unto This Last* to read on the way, saying, 'You will like this book'.

The book was impossible to lay aside once I had begun it. It gripped me. The train reached Durban in the evening. I could not get any sleep that night. This was the first book of Ruskin I had ever read. It brought about an instantaneous and practical transformation in my life. I determined to change my life in accordance with the teachings of the book, which seemed to me

to reflect some of my deepest convictions. These teachings I understood
to be:

> That the good of the individual is contained in the good of all
> That a lawyer's work has the same value as a barber's, inasmuch as all have the same
> right of earning their livelihood from their work
> That a life of labour, that is, the life of the tiller of the soil and the handicraftsman, is
> the life worth living

The first of these I knew.

The second I had dimly realized.

The third had never before occurred to me. *Unto This Last* made it as clear
as daylight that the second and the third were contained in the first. I arose
with the dawn, ready to reduce these principles into practice.

> *Four decades later, Gandhiji affirmed his faith in the teachings of the book when he said in*
> *an interview:*
>
> *'I stand by what is implied in the phrase 'Unto This Last'. That book marked the turning*
> *point in my life. We must do even unto this last as we would have the world do by us.*
> *All must have equal opportunity. Given the opportunity, every human being has the same*
> *possibility for spiritual growth.'*
>
> (CWMG, Vol. 86, p. 21)

> *Defining equality, Gandhiji said:*
>
> *'Equality can never mean uniformity. Equality only means uniformity in justice. There is no*
> *distinction between an atom and the Himalayas in the eyes of god. He is the same to the*
> *atom as to the Himalayas.'*
>
> (CWMG, Vol. 56, p. 104)

The Phoenix Settlement

The very first result of my determination to transform my life was the decision to remove *Indian Opinion* to a farm where everyone should labour, drawing the same wage, and attend to the press in their spare time. Mr West approved of the proposal and £3 was laid down as the monthly allowance per head. I soon advertised for a piece of land situated near a railway station in the vicinity of Durban, and ultimately purchased twenty acres of land with a nice little spring and a few orange and mango trees. Adjoining this was a piece of eighty acres with many fruit trees and a dilapidated cottage. This too was purchased at an aggregate cost of £1,000. A shed was soon erected for the press, and Mr West and others at great personal risk stayed with the carpenters and masons. The place, which was uninhabited and thickly overgrown with grass, was infested with snakes, and was obviously dangerous to live in. We cleared it all and made it habitable, and in about a week we carted most of our things to Phoenix, which gave the name to the settlement. I endeavoured to draw to Phoenix those relations and friends who had come with me from India to try their fortune.

Some of them agreed. Of these I can single out here only the late Maganlal Gandhi's name. He left his business for good to cast in his lot with me, and by his ability, sacrifice, and devotion, he easily stood foremost among my co-workers in my ethical experiments, and as a self-taught handicraftsman his place among them was unique. It was he who led the band which after the conclusion of the South African Satyagraha returned to India and were the original members of the institution which is now known as Satyagraha Ashram. Up to the time of his death in 1928 he was the soul of this institution and practically wore himself away in putting into practice all my cherished principles. His death was an irreparable blow to me.

The Phoenix settlement was thus started in 1904 and in spite of numerous difficulties *Indian Opinion* still continues to be published at the settlement. I need not dilate here on the initial difficulties, the hopes and the disappointments. Though Maganlal Gandhi was new to all the branches of press work, he mastered practically all of them and surpassed us all.

Addressing the inmates of the Satyagraha Ashram at Sabarmati in Ahmedabad, Gandhiji recalled his days at Phoenix:

'In South Africa, my best creation was Phoenix. Without it there would have been no satyagraha in that country. Without the Ashram here, satyagraha will be impossible in India ... Do not attribute greatness to me for other works of mine; judge me only by the Ashram. One of my creations here in the Ashram is Maganlal. If I have found

from experience five million shortcomings in Maganlal, I have found ten million virtues in him.'

(CWMG, Vol. 15, p. 92)

We had hardly settled down when I had to leave the newly constructed nest to go to Johannesburg. Here I informed Polak of the important changes I had made. His joy knew no bounds when he learnt that his book had become for me an epoch-making one. He left his place on the staff of the *Critic* and soon became a member of the family. But I could not keep him there long. It was impossible for me to bear the burden of the Johannesburg office single-handed, and so I suggested to Polak that he should join the office and qualify as an attorney. I had thought that ultimately both of us would retire and settle at Phoenix, but that never came to pass. Work continued to keep me away from Phoenix and I had to satisfy myself with what little I could achieve in rearranging my household in the light of Ruskin's teaching. I introduced as much simplicity as was possible in a barrister's house. The liking for doing all the physical labour increased. Instead of buying baker's bread, we began to prepare unleavened whole meal bread at home. Hand-ground flour was essential for this, and to this end, I invested in a hand-worked flour-mill for £7. It could be worked by two, and Polak and I and the children usually worked it. The children liked and seemed to flourish on this exercise. Though we had a servant and the municipal sweeper removed the nightsoil, we personally attended to the cleaning of the closets instead of expecting the servant to do it. This proved a good training for the children, with the result that none of my sons developed any aversion for scavenger's work, and they naturally got a good grounding in sanitation.

Whilst I was thus disciplining myself and the children, an event occurred which helped me to decide to break up the Johannesburg home, and send my wife and children to go and settle at Phoenix, Mr Polak taking up a smaller house for himself. This event was the outbreak of what was officially described as the Zulu 'Rebellion'.

The Zulu 'Rebellion'

The Zulu 'Rebellion', like the Boer War, was another occasion on which I was impelled more by a sense of loyalty to the British Empire than anything else, to offer what service I could render. I bore no grudge against the Zulus; they had harmed no Indian. I would not have described the rising as 'rebellion', but the British Empire then, in my opinion, existed for the welfare of the world, and as a citizen of Natal, which was part of the Empire, I felt bound to write to the Governor offering to form an Indian Ambulance Corps. The offer was readily accepted and I forthwith went to Durban and appealed for recruits. We were a party of twenty-four and I was made temporary Sergeant-Major in order to give me a status. Our corps was on active service for nearly six weeks. On reaching the scene of the 'rebellion' I saw that it was nothing but a no-tax campaign. My heart was with the Zulus and I was delighted to hear that our main work was to be the nursing of wounded Zulus. The Medical Officer who was at his wits' end for want of men to take up the work, as no white people were forthcoming for the purpose, hailed our arrival with delight. He immediately armed us with bandages, disinfectants, etc., and took us to the improvised hospital. The Zulus were filled with joy and gratefulness to have our service. The wounded in our charge were not wounded in battle. A section of them had been taken prisoners as suspects. The General had sentenced them to be flogged, and the flogging had caused severe sores. The others were Zulu friendlies. We were attached to a swift-moving column which had orders to march wherever danger was reported. Twice or thrice we had to march forty miles a day. But wherever we went, I am thankful that we had God's good work to do, having to carry to the camp on our stretchers, the Zulu friendlies who had been inadvertently wounded and to attend on them as nurses.

The 'rebellion' was no war but seemed to me to be a manhunt; many Englishmen whom I met thought likewise. To hear every morning reports of the soldiers' rifles exploding like crackers in innocent hamlets, and to live in the midst of them was a trial. But I swallowed the bitter draught and salved my conscience by the thought that we were privileged to attend to the wounded Zulus who but for us would have been uncared for.

A Life Plunge

But if my conscience was thus eased, there was much else to set one thinking. Marching with or without the wounded through the solemn hills and dales of Zululand, I often fell into deep thought. I pondered over brahmacharya and its implications and my convictions took deeper root. I discussed it with co-workers. I had not then realized how indispensable it was for self-realization, but I clearly saw that one aspiring to serve humanity with his whole soul could not do without it. It was borne upon me that I should have more and more occasions for service of the kind I was rendering, and that I should find myself unequal to my task if I were engaged in the pleasures of family life and in the propagation and rearing of children.

In a word, I could not live both after the flesh and the spirit. On the present occasion, for instance, I should not have been able to throw myself into the fray, had my wife been expecting a baby. Without the observance of brahmacharya there would be a conflict between the service of the family and the service of humanity. With brahmacharya they would be perfectly consistent.

Whilst I was thus in the midst of strenuous physical and mental work, a report came to the effect that the work of suppressing the 'rebellion' was nearly over and we should be soon discharged. The discharge came in a day or two, followed by a letter from the Governor specially thanking us for our services.

On arrival at Phoenix and after discussion with co-workers, I took the final plunge, namely, the vow of brahmacharya for life. I must confess that I had not then fully realized the magnitude and immensity of the undertaking. But I was fortified by the conviction that a solemn vow was like being with one's back to the wall.

I rejected all the seductive objections against a permanent vow. An abiding vow is like a fortress affording protection against dangerous temptations. It cures one of weakness and vacillation. Well has the poet sung: 'Renunciation without aversion cannot last'. During the transition process whilst aversion for evil things grows, a vow is a vital necessity.

I had not shared my thoughts with my wife until I took the vow in 1906. To my great joy and to her lasting credit she raised no objection.

The freedom and joy that came to me after taking the vow had never been experienced before 1906. In about a month after this the foundation of satyagraha was laid. As though unknown to me, the brahmacharya vow had been preparing me for it. Satyagraha had not been a preconceived plan. It came on spontaneously without my having willed it. But I could see that all my previous steps had led up to that goal. I had cut down my heavy household expenses at Johannesburg and gone to Phoenix to take, as it were, the brahmacharya vow.

But if it was a matter of ever-increasing joy, let no one believe that it was an easy thing for me. Even in my old age I realize how hard a thing it is. Every day I realize more and more that it is like walking on the sword's edge and I see every moment the necessity for eternal vigilance.

Brahmacharya means control of all the senses in thought, word and deed. It is well to realize the distinction between the life of *a brahmachari* and of a libertine. Both use their eyesight, but whereas the brahmachari uses it to see the glories of God, the other uses it to see the frivolity around him. Both use their ears, but whereas the one hears nothing but praises of God, the other feasts his ears on vulgar and idle gossip. Both often keep late hours, but whereas the one devotes them to meditation and prayer, the other fritters them away in wild and wasteful mirth. Both feed the inner man, but the one does so only to keep the temple of God in good repair, and the other gorges himself and makes the sacred vessel a muck-heap.

Such brahmacharya is impossible of attainment except by ceaseless and tireless effort. But those who desire to observe brahmacharya with a view to realizing God need not despair, provided their faith in God is equal to their confidence in their own effort.

> 'Electricity is a great force but all cannot benefit from it. There are certain laws for generating it and therefore we can get electricity only if we abide by those laws. Electricity is a lifeless force. Men, the living beings, have to labour hard to acquire the knowledge of its laws.
>
> 'Similarly there are laws for knowing the great living force which we call God. But it is self-evident that it requires hard labour to find out those laws. That law in short is termed brahmacharya.
>
> 'The current meaning of brahmacharya is complete control over the sex organs. The golden means to attain that end is Ramanama.'
>
> (CWMG, Vol. 88, p. 149)

As the Gita says: 'The sense-objects turn away from an abstemious soul, leaving intact the relish for them. The relish too disappears with the realization of the Highest.' Therefore His name and His grace are the last resources of the aspirant after moksha (salvation). This truth came to me only after my return to India.

Some Reminiscences of the Bar

I may recall in this chapter one or two of my experiences during my practice as a lawyer in South Africa. As a student I had heard that the lawyer's profession was a liar's profession. But this did not influence me, as I had no intention of earning either position or money by lying. So far as I can recollect I never resorted to untruth in my profession, and a large part of my legal practice was in the interest of public work, for which I charged nothing beyond out-of-pocket expenses, and those too I sometimes met myself. In fixing my fees I do not recall ever having made them conditional on my winning the case. I warned every new client at the outset that he should not expect me to take up a false case or to coach the witnesses, with the result that I built up such a reputation that no false cases would come to me.

On one occasion whilst I was conducting a case before a magistrate in Johannesburg I discovered that my client had deceived me. I saw him completely break down in the witness box. So without any argument I asked the magistrate to dismiss the case. The opposing counsel was astonished and the magistrate was pleased. My conduct in this case did not affect my practice for the worse, indeed it made my work easier. I also saw that my devotion to truth enhanced my reputation amongst the members of the profession, and in spite of the handicap of colour I was able, in some cases, to win even their affection.

On one occasion the late Parsi Rustomji, whose name is a household word amongst the Indians in South Africa, got into a very bad scrape. He had long been my co-worker and used to keep me informed of his affairs. But this time he had kept me in the dark. He was a large importer of goods from Bombay and Calcutta, and he had occasionally resorted to smuggling. He was on the best terms with the Customs officials and no one was inclined to suspect him. But on this particular occasion his invoice was questioned and his guilt discovered. He came running to me, contrite and penitent, the tears rolling down his cheeks. I calmed him and assured him that there was only one way of being saved that I knew, namely, a clean confession.

'But is not my confession before you enough?' he asked.

'You have wronged not me, but the Government. How will the confession made before me avail you?' I replied.

We consulted his counsel, who did not seem inclined to fall in with my suggestion, but Parsi Rustomji preferred to be guided by me. I offered to meet both the Customs officer and the Attorney-General, with whom it rested to initiate the prosecution, and proposed that Parsi Rustomji should offer to pay the penalty they might fix; if they were not agreeable, Parsi Rustomji should go to jail. The shame, I explained to him, lay not so much in going to jail as in committing the offence.

I cannot say that Parsi Rustomji took this all in at once. But he was a brave man. 'Well,' he said, 'I have told you already that I am entirely in your hands.'

I brought all my powers of persuasion to bear on this case. I met both the officials concerned. They appreciated my complete frankness and were convinced that I had kept back nothing. The case against Parsi Rustomji was compromised. He was to pay a penalty equal to twice the amount he had confessed to have smuggled. Sheth Rustomji reduced to writing the facts of the whole case, got the paper framed, and hung it up in his office to serve as a perpetual reminder to his heirs and fellow-merchants.

The Birth of Satyagraha

On return from duty in the Zulu 'rebellion', whilst I was discussing with my co-workers at Phoenix my plans and life's ideals, news reached me of a draft Ordinance published in the *Transvaal Government Gazette Extraordinary* of 22 August 1906. It meant ruin for the Indians in South Africa.

Under it, every Indian, man, woman or child of eight years or upwards, entitled to reside in the Transvaal, had to register his or her name with the Registrar of Asiatics and take out a certificate of registration.

The applicants for registration had to surrender their old permits to the Registrar, and state in their applications their names, residence, caste, age, etc. The Registrar was to note down important marks of identification upon the applicant's person, and take his finger and thumb impressions. Every Indian who failed thus to apply for registration before a certain date was to forfeit his right of residence in the Transvaal. Failure to apply would be held to be an offence in law for which the defaulter could be fined, sent to prison or even deported within the discretion of the court.

Soon there was held a small meeting of the leading Indians, to whom I explained the Ordinance word by word. It shocked them as it had shocked me. All present realized the seriousness of the situation and resolved to hold a public meeting.

The meeting was duly held on 11 September 1906. The most important among the resolutions passed by the meeting was the famous Fourth Resolution. I fully explained to the meeting this resolution whereby the audience solemnly determined not to submit to the Ordinance in the event of its becoming law in the teeth of their opposition and to suffer all the penalties attaching to such non-submission. This movement, for the moment described as 'passive resistance', soon came to be known as 'Satyagraha'.

> 'Satyagraha was born in South Africa in 1908. There was no word in any Indian language denoting the power which our countrymen in South Africa evoked for the redress of their grievances. There was an English equivalent, namely "passive resistance", and we carried on with it. However, the need for a word to describe this unique power came to be increasingly felt, and it was decided to award a prize to anyone who could think of an appropriate term. A Gujarati-speaking gentleman submitted the word "satyagraha", and it was judged the best.

> 'Passive resistance conveyed the idea of the Suffragette Movement in England. Burning of houses by these women was called "passive resistance" and so also their fasting in prison. All such acts might very well be "passive resistance" but they were not "satyagraha"... The movement in South Africa was not passive but active ... Satyagraha is not physical force. A satyagrahi does not inflict pain on the adversary; he does not seek his destruction. A satyagrahi does not resort to firearms. In the use of satyagraha, there is no ill will whatever.

> 'Satyagraha is pure soul-force. Truth is the very substance of the soul. That is why this force is called satyagraha. The soul is informed with knowledge. In it burns the flame of love. If someone gives us pain through ignorance, we shall win him through love. Non-violence is the supreme dharma. [It] is the proof of love.'

> (CWMG, Vol. 13, pp. 520–1)

We were unable to prevent the Ordinance passing into law, and in spite of picketing and public opinion, some few Indians registered themselves. But when the Asiatic Department found that all their exertions notwithstanding, they could not get more than 500 Indians willing to register, they decided to arrest someone or other. In Germiston there lived many Indians, one of whom was Pandit Rama Sundara. This man had a brave look and was endowed with some gift of the gab. Till yesterday known only to the good people of Germiston, he became famous as soon as he was arrested. In the court too Rama Sundara was accorded due respect, not as an ordinary prisoner but as a representative of his community. Eager Indian spectators filled the courtroom. Rama Sundara was sentenced to a month's simple imprisonment, and kept in a separate cell in the European ward in Johannesburg jail. The day on which he was sentenced was celebrated with great éclat.

But Rama Sundara turned out to be a false coin. In spite of all the attention showered upon him by the jail authorities as well as by the community, imprisonment appeared irksome to him and he bade a final goodbye to the Transvaal and to the movement.

I have referred to the story of Rama Sundara not in order to expose his faults, but to point a moral. The leaders of every clean movement are bound to see that they admit only clean fighters to it.

Imprisoned

But the Government failed to reap any advantage from Rama Sundara's arrest. On the other hand they observed the spirit of the Indian community rising higher. The officers of the Asiatic Department were diligent readers of *Indian Opinion*. Secrecy had been deliberately ruled out of the movement. So the paper became for the officers a faithful mirror of the current history of the movement. They thus came to think the strength of the movement could not by any means be broken so long as certain leaders were at large. Some of the leading men were consequently served with a notice in the Christmas week of 1907 to appear before the Magistrate. All of them appeared before the court on the date specified, Saturday 28 December 1907, to showcause why, having failed to apply for registration, as required by law, they should not be ordered to leave the Transvaal within a given period.

The Magistrate conducted each case separately, and ordered all the accused to leave the Transvaal within forty-eight hours in some cases and seven or fourteen days in others.

The time limit expired on 10 January 1908 and the same day we were called upon to attend court for sentence.

None of us had to offer any defence. All were to plead guilty to the charge of disobeying the order to leave the Transvaal within the stated period.

In the statement that I was allowed to make before the court I asked the Magistrate to impose upon me the heaviest penalty. The Magistrate, however, did not accede to my request and sentenced me to two months' simple imprisonment. I had some slight feeling of awkwardness due to the fact that I was standing as an accused in the very court where I had often appeared as counsel. But I well remember that I considered the former role as far more honourable than the latter, and felt proud of entering the prisoner's box.

In the court there were hundreds of Indians as well as brother members of the Bar in front of me. On the sentence being pronounced I was at once removed in custody and was then quite alone. The policeman asked me to sit on a bench kept there for prisoners, shut the door on me and went away. I was somewhat agitated and fell into deep thought. Home, the courts where I practised, the public meeting—all these passed away like a dream, and I was now a prisoner. What will happen in two months? Shall I have to serve the full term? If the people courted imprisonment in large numbers, as they had promised, there would be no question of serving the full sentence. But if they failed to fill the prisons, two months would be as tedious as an age. These thoughts passed through my mind in less than one-hundredth of the time that it has taken me to dictate them. And they filled me with shame. How vain I was! I, who had asked the people to consider the prisons as His Majesty's hotels, the suffering consequent upon disobeying the Black Act as perfect bliss, and the sacrifice of one's all and of life itself in resisting it as supreme enjoyment! Where had all this knowledge vanished today? This second train of thought acted upon me as a bracing tonic, and I began to laugh at my own folly. I began to think what kind of imprisonment would be awarded to the others and whether they would be kept with me in the prison. But the train of thought was disturbed by the police officer who opened the gate and asked me to follow him, which I did. He then made me go before him, following me himself, took me to the prisoners' closed van and asked me to take my seat in it. I was driven to Johannesburg jail.

In jail I was asked to take off my own private clothing. After the officers had recorded my name and address, I was taken to a large cell, and in a short time was joined by my compatriots who came laughing and told me how they had received the same sentence as myself, and what took place after I had been removed. We were all happy at the thought that we were kept in the same jail and in the same cell.

First Jail Experiences

The cell door was locked at 6 o'clock. The door had no bars but was quite solid, there being high up in the wall a small aperture for ventilation, so that we felt as if we had been locked up in a safe.

From the second or third day, Satyagrahi prisoners began to arrive in large numbers. They had all courted arrest and most of them were hawkers. In South Africa, every hawker, black or white, had to take out a licence, always carry it with him and show it to the police when asked to do so. Nearly every day someone would be asked to show the licence, and those who had none to show would be arrested. The community had resolved to fill up the jail after our arrests. In this the hawkers took the lead. It was easy for them to be arrested. They only had to refuse to show their licences and that was enough to ensure their arrest. In this way the number of satyagrahi prisoners swelled to more than a hundred in one week. And as some few were sure to arrive every day, we received the daily quota of news without a newspaper. When satyagrahis began to be arrested in large numbers, they were sentenced to imprisonment with hard labour.

In Johannesburg jail prisoners not condemned to hard labour got 'mealie pap' in the morning. There was no salt in it, but each prisoner was given some salt separately. At noon the prisoners were given four ounces of rice, four ounces of bread, one ounce of ghee and a little salt, and in the evening, 'mealie pap' and some vegetable, chiefly potatoes of which two were given if they were small and only one if they were big in size. None of us was satisfied with this diet. The rice was cooked too soft. We asked the medical officer for some condiments, and told him that condiments were allowed in the jails in India. 'This is not India,' was the stern answer. 'There is no question of relish about prison diet and condiments therefore cannot be allowed.' We asked for pulse on the ground that the regulation diet was lacking in muscle-building properties. 'Prisoners must not indulge in arguments on medical grounds,' replied the doctor. 'You do get muscle-building food, as twice a week you are served boiled beans instead of maize.' The doctor's argument was sound if the human stomach was capable of extracting the various elements out of various foods taken at various times in a week or fortnight. As a matter of fact he had no intention whatever of looking to our

convenience. The Superintendent permitted us to cook our food ourselves. We elected Thambi Naidoo as our chef, and as such he had to fight many a battle on our behalf. If the vegetable ration issued was short in weight, he would insist on getting full weight. On vegetable days, which were two in a week, we cooked twice and on other days only once, as we were allowed to cook other things for ourselves only for the noon-day meal. We were somewhat better off after we began to cook our own food.

But whether or not we succeeded in obtaining these conveniences, every one of us was firm in his resolution of passing his term in jail in perfect happiness and peace. The number of satyagrahi prisoners gradually rose to over 150.

We had thus been in jail for a fortnight, when fresh arrivals brought the news that the Government was busy considering the possibility of a compromise with the Indians. I was summoned to see General Smuts, and it was proposed that the prisoners should be released and the 'Black Act' withdrawn if a sufficient number of Indians would register voluntarily. As a satyagrahi I could not reject such a compromise. The prisoners were released, and I set about explaining the terms of the settlement to my countrymen.

A Memorable Episode

I

I went straight to Johannesburg and the meeting was held that very night at about 11 or 12 pm. The audience numbered nearly a thousand, in spite of the shortness of the notice and the late hour. The meeting unanimously ratified the settlement with the exception of a couple of Pathans, for the Pathans would not be convinced that it was right for them to give their fingerprints even voluntarily.

On the morning of 10th February 1908 some of us got ready to go and take our certificates of registration. The supreme necessity of getting through the registration business with all possible expedition had been fully impressed on the community, and it had been agreed that the leaders should be the first to take out certificates, with a view to break down hesitation and to see if the officers concerned discharged their duties with courtesy, and generally to keep an eye on all the arrangements.

When I reached my office, which was also the office of the Satyagraha Association, I found Mir Alam, a Pathan, standing with some friends outside the premises. Mir Alam was an old client of mine, and used to seek my advice in all his affairs. He was fully six feet in height and of a large and powerful build. That day for the first time I saw Mir Alam outside my office instead of inside it, and although his eyes met mine, he for the first time refrained from saluting me. I saluted him and he saluted me in return. As usual I asked him, 'How do you do?', and my impression is that he said he was all right. But he did not that day wear his usual smile. I noticed his angry eyes and took a mental note of the fact. I thought that something was going to happen. I entered the office. The Chairman, Mr Essop Mian, and other friends arrived, and we set out for the Asiatic Office. Mir Alam and his companions followed us.

The Registration Office was at Von Brandis Square, less than a mile away from my office, and the way to it led through main roads. As we were going along Von Brandis Street, outside the premises of Messrs. Arnot and Gibson, not more than three minutes' walk from the Registration Office, Mir Alam accosted me and asked me, 'Where are you going?'

'I propose to take out a certificate of registration, giving the ten fingerprints,' I replied. 'If you will go with me, I will first get you a certificate, with an impression only of the two thumbs, and then I will take one for myself, giving the fingerprints.'

I had scarcely finished the last sentence when a heavy cudgel blow descended on my head from behind. I at once fainted with the words '*He Rama*' on my lips, lay prostrate on the ground and had no notion of what followed.

> *Nearly forty years later, on 30 January 1948, Gandhiji who ever had Lord Rama in his mind and heart, fell to an assassin's bullet with the words 'He Rama' on his lips. A detailed account is given in the footnote in CWMG, Vol. 90, p. 536.*

But Mir Alam and his companions gave me more blows and kicks. The noise attracted some European passers-by to the scene. Mir Alam and his companions fled, but were caught by the Europeans. The police arrived in the meanwhile and took them in custody. I was picked up and carried into Mr J. C. Gibson's private office. When I regained consciousness, I saw my friend Mr Doke bending over me. 'How do you feel?' he asked me.

'I am all right,' I replied, 'but there is pain in the teeth and the ribs. Where is Mir Alam?'

'He has been arrested along with the rest.'

'They should be released,' said I.

'That is all very well. But here you are in a stranger's office with your lip and cheek badly cut. The police are ready to take you to the hospital, but if you will go to my place, Mrs Doke and I will minister to your comforts as best we can.'

'Yes, I should love to go to your place. Please thank the police for their offer but tell them that I prefer to go with you.'

Mr Chamney the Registrar of Asiatics too now arrived on the scene. I was taken in a carriage to this good clergyman's residence in Smit Street and a doctor was called in. Meanwhile I said to Mr Chamney: 'I wished to come to your office, give ten fingerprints and take out the first certificate of registration, but God willed it otherwise. However, I have now to request you to bring the papers and allow me to register at once. I hope that you will not let anyone else register before me.'

'Where is the hurry about it?' asked Mr Chamney. 'The doctor will be here soon. You please rest and all will be well. I will issue certificates to others but keep your name at the head of the list.'

'Not so,' I replied. 'I am pledged to take out the first certificate if I am alive and if it is acceptable to God. It is therefore that I would like the papers brought here and now.'

Upon this Mr Chamney fetched the papers.

The second thing for me to do was to wire to the Attorney-General that I did not hold Mir Alam and others guilty of the assault committed upon me, that in any case I did not wish them to be prosecuted and that I hoped they would be discharged for my sake. He and his companions were thereupon released. But the Europeans of Johannesburg addressed a strong letter to the Attorney-General saying that whatever views Gandhi might hold as regards the punishment of criminals, they could not be put into effect in South Africa. Gandhi himself might not take any steps, but the assault was committed not in a private place but on the high road and was therefore a public offence. Several Englishmen too were in a position to tender evidence and the offenders must be prosecuted. Upon this the Attorney-General re-arrested Mir Alam and one of his companions. They were sentenced to three months' hard labour. But I was not summoned as a witness.

A Memorable Episode

II

Let us return to the sick-room. Dr Thwaites came in while Mr Chamney was still away. He examined me and stitched up the wounds on the upper lip. He prescribed some medicine to be applied to the ribs and enjoined silence upon me so long as the stitches were not removed.

Thus speech was forbidden me, but I was still master of my hands. I addressed a short note as follows to the community through the Chairman and sent it for publication:

> I am well in the brotherly and sisterly hands of Mr and Mrs Doke. I hope to take up my duty shortly. Those who have committed the act did not know what they were doing. They thought that I was doing what was wrong. They have had their redress in the only manner they know. I therefore request that no steps be taken against them. Seeing that the assault was committed by a Mussalman or Mussalmans, the Hindus might probably feel hurt. If so, they would put themselves in the wrong before the world and their Maker. Rather let the blood spilt today cement the two communities indissolubly—such is my heartfelt prayer. May God grant it. Assault or no assault, my advice remains the same. The large majority of Asiatics ought to give fingerprints. Those who have real conscientious scruples will be exempted by the Government. To ask for more would be to betray childishness. The spirit of satyagraha rightly understood should make the people fear none but God. No cowardly fear therefore should deter the vast majority of sober-minded

Indians from doing their duty. The promise of repeal of the Act against voluntary registration having been given, it is the sacred duty of every good Indian to help the Government and the Colony to the uttermost.

Mr Chamney returned with the papers and, though extremely weak, I managed somehow to give my fingerprints. I then saw that tears stood in Mr Chamney's eyes. I had often to write bitterly against him, but this showed me how man's heart may be softened by events.

Mr Doke and his good wife were anxious that I should be perfectly at rest and peaceful, and were therefore pained to witness my mental activity after the assault. They were afraid that it might react in a manner prejudicial to my health. They, therefore, quietly removed all persons from near my bed, and asked me not to write or do anything. I made a request in writing, that in order to induce restfulness, their daughter Olive, who was then only a little girl, should sing for me my favourite English hymn, 'Lead, kindly light'. Mr Doke readily acceded to my request. The whole scene passes before my eyes as I picture myself to Olive stealthily standing near the door and softly singing the hymn. The melodious voice of little Olive still reverberates in my ears.

In a letter of 1932 to his good friend Verrier Elwin, Gandhiji wrote:

'...today being Friday, without any prompting from me, Mahadev gave effect to your suggestion about fellowship by singing "Lead Kindly Light" in its very beautiful Gujarati version. At the evening service, it is always Mahadev's part to sing the bhajan. The hour would be approximately 7.40. The prayer commences at 7.30 and opens with the 19 verses at the end of the second discourse of the Gita. It is followed by Ramanama, and then comes the bhajan. As soon as I read your suggestion, I had no hesitation in endorsing it, but I was debating as to the choice of the hymn. I had in mind the singing of the English text and so the choice was limited. It could either be "Lead Kindly Light" or "When I Survey the Wondrous Cross" or "Take my Life and Let It Be" for the simple reason that I cannot very well sing any of the other favourite hymns of mine—not even these three I sing accurately... Mahadev is unused to the tune of English hymns, but by taking up the Gujarati version of "Lead Kindly Light", Mahadev solved the difficulty about the choice and the singing. There is a special fitness about the choice of this hymn and Newman's. It was that hymn which, when I was in physical distress, was sung by Olive Doke in Johannesburg under the late Rev. Doke's roof. So you may take it that we will be singing this hymn at 7.40 every Friday evening, with the knowledge that you at least will be joining us wherever you are, whether the suggestion is taken up or not by the other friends.

(CWMG, Vol. 49, pp. 485–6)

Satyagraha Resumed

We have seen in the last chapter how the Indians registered voluntarily to the satisfaction of the Transvaal Government. The Government were now to repeal the Black Act, and if they did, the satyagraha struggle would come to an end. But instead of repealing the Black Act, General Smuts took a fresh step forward. He maintained the Black Act on the statute book and introduced into the Legislature a measure, validating the voluntary registrations effected and 'making further provision for the registration of Asiatics'. I was simply astounded when I read the Bill.

I wrote a letter to General Smuts, but politicians do not reply at all to embarrassing questions, or if they do, they resort to circumlocution.

We therefore sent a firm letter to the Transvaal Government saying, in effect: 'If the Asiatic Act is not repealed in terms of the settlement, and if the Government's decision to that effect is not communicated to the Indians before a specific date, the certificates collected by the Indians will be burnt, and we shall humbly but firmly take the consequences.'

The ultimatum was to expire on the same day that the new Asiatic Bill was to be carried through the Legislature. A meeting had been called some two hours after the expiry of the time limit to perform the public ceremony of burning the certificates. The Satyagraha Committee thought that the meeting would not be fruitless even if quite unexpectedly perhaps a favourable reply was received from the Government, as in that case the meeting could be utilized for announcing the Government's favourable decision to the community.

As the business of the meeting was about to commence, a volunteer arrived on a cycle with a telegram from the Government in which they regretted the determination of the Indian community and announced their inability to change their line of action. The telegram was read to the audience which

received it with cheers, as if they were glad that the auspicious opportunity of burning the certificates did not after all slip out of their hands.

The meeting began. The Chairman put the meeting on their guard and explained the whole situation to them. Appropriate resolutions were adopted.

The Committee had already received upwards of 2,000 certificates to be burnt. These were all thrown into a cauldron, saturated with paraffin and set ablaze. The whole assembly rose to their feet and made the place resound with the echoes of their continuous cheers over the bonfire. Some of those who had still withheld their certificates brought them in numbers to the platform to be thrown into the cauldron.

The press reporters present at the meeting were profoundly impressed with the whole scene and gave graphic descriptions of the meeting in their papers.

During the same year in which the Black Act was passed, 1907, General Smuts carried through the Legislature another Bill called the Transvaal Immigrants Restriction Bill. This Act indirectly prevented the entry of a single Indian newcomer into the Transvaal.

It was absolutely essential for the Indians to resist this fresh inroad on their rights. During the next two years many satyagrahis from the neighbouring Colony of Natal voluntarily entered the Transvaal, and were consequently imprisoned at the border township of Volksrust. Desirous of joining these helpers from Natal, many enthusiasts who had burnt their certificates started hawking vegetables in the streets, for which a certificate was necessary, and got themselves arrested. At one time there were as many as seventy-five Indians in the Volksrust jail. The Government became worried at the persistence of these satyagrahis whom prison did not deter, and they began to deport offenders instead of imprisoning them: this caused some Indians to weaken, but many remained perfectly firm and cheerful and continued the struggle.

Tolstoy Farm

Till now (1910), we had been supporting the families of jail-going men by monthly cash allowances. This proved to be unsatisfactory and wasteful of the public funds. And where were the men who constantly went to jail to live in their intervals of freedom? For no one would employ them. There was only one solution to these two difficulties, namely, that all the satyagrahis and their families should live together and become members of a sort of cooperative commonwealth.

Mr Kallenbach, who has been already introduced to the reader, generously gave us the use of a farm of 1,100 acres, free of charge.

> In this abridged story, however, the name of Kallenbach occurs for the first time.
>
> Of Kallenbach, a prosperous German architect of Johannesburg, Gandhiji said:
> 'He is a German and a soldier, but I feel that no purer-minded person today walks the earth in Europe.' He would describe Kallenbach as 'a man of strong feelings, wide sympathies and childlike simplicity.'

Upon the farm there were nearly one thousand fruit-bearing trees and a small house at the foot of a hill with accommodation for half a dozen persons. Water was supplied from two wells and from a spring. The nearest railway station, Lawley, was about a mile from the farm and Johannesburg twenty-one miles. We decided to build houses upon this farm and to invite the families of satyagrahis to settle there. Upon the farm oranges, apricots and plums grew in such abundance that during the season the satyagrahis could have their fill of the fruit and yet have a surplus. The spring was about 500 yards away from our quarters. We insisted that we should not have any servants whether for the household work or even for the farming and building operations. Everything therefore, from cooking to scavenging, was done with our own hands. As regards accommodating women, we had resolved from the first that they should be housed separately. The houses therefore were to be built in two separate blocks, each at some distance from the other. For the time it was considered sufficient to provide accommodation for ten women and sixty men. Then again we had to erect a house for Mr Kallenbach and by its side a school house, as well as a workshop for carpentry, shoemaking, etc.

The settlers hailed from Gujarat, Tamilnad, Andhrapradesh and north India, and there were Hindus, Mussalmans, Parsis and Christians among them. About forty of them were young men, two or three old men, five women and twenty to thirty children, of whom four or five were girls.

The weak became strong on Tolstoy Farm and labour proved to be a tonic for all.

Everyone wanted to go to Johannesburg now and then. Children used to like going there just for a spree. I had to go there on business. We therefore made a rule that one could go there by rail only on public business and then too travel third class. Anyone who wanted to go for pleasure must walk and carry home-made provisions with him. None could spend anything on his food in the city. Had it not been

for these drastic rules, the money saved by living in a rural locality would
have been wasted in railway fares and eating-houses. The provisions carried
were the simplest: home-baked bread made from coarse wholemeal ground at
home, groundnut butter also prepared at home, and home-made marmalade.
We made our own flour as we had an iron hand-mill for grinding wheat.
Groundnut butter was made by baking and then pounding groundnuts, and
was four times cheaper than ordinary butter. As for the oranges, we had
plenty of them on the farm. We scarcely used cow's milk on the farm and
generally managed with condensed milk.

But to return to the Johannesburg trips. Anyone who wished to go to
Johannesburg went there on foot once or twice a week and returned the
same day. As I have already stated, it was a journey of twenty-one miles to
and fro. We saved hundreds of rupees by this one rule of going on foot, and
those who thus went walking were much benefited. Some newly acquired
the habit of walking. The general practice was that the sojourner should rise
at two o'clock and start at half past two. He would reach Johannesburg in six
to seven hours. The record for the minimum time taken on the journey was
4 hours 18 minutes.

As the idea was to make the farm a busy hive, and thus to make it partially
pay its way so that we could battle with the Government indefinitely if
necessary, we had a little shoe factory. There was close by a monastery of
German Catholic monks where one could go and learn the art of making
sandals. Mr Kallenbach went there and acquired the art. He taught it to
me, and I, in my turn, to other workers. I remember having made dozens
of pairs myself, though many of the youngsters surpassed me. We sold the
sandals to our friends and made some money. We also introduced carpentry,
and made all manner of things large and small, from benches to boxes.

A school was indispensable for the settlement. This was the most difficult
of our tasks and we never achieved complete success in this matter till the

very last. The burden of teaching work was largely borne by Mr Kallenbach and myself. The school could be held only after noon, when both of us were thoroughly exhausted by our morning labour, and so were our pupils. The teachers therefore would often be dozing, as well as the taught. We would sprinkle water on the eyes, and by playing with the children try to pull them up and to pull up ourselves, but sometimes in vain. The body peremptorily demanded rest and would not take a denial. But this was only one and the least of our many difficulties. For the classes were conducted in spite of these dozings. What were we to teach pupils speaking three different languages, Gujarati, Tamil or Telugu, and how? I was anxious to make the vernacular the medium of instruction.

> In 1915, back in India, Gandhiji recalled in a public speech, one of Kallenabach's other skills, namely, his proficiency at the game of quoits.
>
> Gandhiji, along with Gokhale and Kallenbach, had sailed on the steamer R.P.D. KRONPRINZ from 18 to 28 November in 1912. Referring to it, he said:
>
> 'Mr Kallenbach ... was accepted as a worthy companion by Mr Gokhale, who used to play with him the game of quoits. Mr Gokhale had just then, during the voyage from England to Cape Town, picked up that game and he very nearly gave Mr Kallenbach a beating in the game ... Mr Kallenbach, as far as I am aware, is one of the cleverest players of quoits in South Africa ... Mr Gokahle ... thought I never indulged in such sports and that I was against them. He expostulated in kind words and said, "Do you know why I want to enter into such competition with Europeans? I certainly want to do at least as much as they can do for the sake of our country. It is said, rightly or wrongly, that we are inferior people in many matters, and so far as I can do it—and this he said in all humility—"I certainly want to show that we are at least their equals, if not their superiors."'
>
> (CWMG, Vol. 13, pp. 116–7)

I knew a little Tamil but no Telugu. What could one teacher do in these circumstances?

But this teaching experiment was not fruitless. The children were saved from the infection of intolerance, and learnt to view one another's religions and customs with a large-hearted charity. They learnt how to live together like children of the same parents. They imbibed the lessons of mutual service, courtesy and industry. And from what little I know about the later activities

of some of the children on Tolstoy Farm, I am certain that the education
which they received there has not been in vain. Even if imperfect, it was a
well-thought-out experiment, with the religious spirit in the background,
and among the sweetest reminiscences of Tolstoy Farm, those of this teaching
experiment are no less sweet than the rest.

> '... most of all we should urge the study of Indian languages, because without a knowledge
> of one's own mother tongue, it is impossible to be a true patriot; one's ideas become warped
> and our hearts estranged from the Motherland. The religions and literature of India can
> never be appreciated through the medium of a foreign language.' (CWMG, Vol. 11, p. 353)
>
> In 1922, Gandhiji wrote a primer on education which was published in 1951 in the
> Gujarati language under the title Balpothi. About the primer Gandhiji said,
>
> 'I have followed in writing this, exactly the same method by which I used to teach the
> children at Tolstoy Farm and other places. I used to act the "mother" there.'

> Further, in his Foreword to the pamphlet, Gandhiji wrote:
>
> 'This primer presupposes that the pupil has already spent a year or less in spinning,
> learning the letters of the alphabet, both Devanagri and Prakrit, and simple tables.
>
> 'I have used in the primer the words "laghushanka" and "apaman" because I could not avoid
> them. I have used the word "laghushanka" in place of peshab, thinking that it would be good
> if children used this fine word. "Apaman" has been kept, as a milder word could not be found.
>
> 'The presentation of the lessons in this primer in the form of dialogue between a mother
> and a child has a touch of artificiality about it, as most mothers today do not perform
> their duty of instructing children, nor are they equipped for the task.'

> (CWMG, Vol. 23, pp. 122–3)

The Women's Part I

In the winter of 1912, Gokhale paid a visit to South Africa to act as mediator between the satyagrahis and the Government. After he had seen General Botha he encouraged us to believe that all would be well. 'Next year,' he said, 'the Black Act will be repealed and the £3 tax abolished.'

But the next year's legislation did nothing to relieve us, and 1913 saw the inhabitants of Tolstoy Farm preparing to renew the satyagraha struggle, with the abolition of the £3 tax as our objective.

So far, although they had often been eager to follow their husbands to jail, we had dissuaded women from courting imprisonment, but as though to strengthen our cause, the South African Government chose this time to enforce a judgment which nullified all marriages that had not been celebrated according to Christian rites or registered by the Registrar of Marriages. Thus in a stroke all marriages celebrated according to the Hindu, Mussalman and Zoroastrian rites were made illegal, and practically all the Indian women in South Africa ceased to be their husbands' legal wives. We felt justified after this in letting the women too fight in a cause that had become of such vital importance to them.

The crisis now arrived, brooking no delay. Patience was impossible in the face of this insult offered to our womankind. We decided to offer stubborn satyagraha irrespective of the number of fighters. Not only could the women now not be prevented from joining the struggle, but, we decided even to invite them to come into line along with the men. We first invited the sisters who had lived on Tolstoy Farm. I found that they were only too glad to enter the struggle. I gave them an idea of the risks incidental to such participation. I explained to them that they would have to put up with restraints in the matter of food, dress, and personal movements. I warned them that they might be given hard work in jail, made to wash clothes and even subjected to insult by the warders. But these sisters were all brave and feared none of these things. One of them was with child, while six of them had young babies in arms. But one and all were eager to join. It was an offence to enter Natal from the Transvaal and vice versa. Our plan was to send a band of volunteers to the Transvaal from Natal where they would probably be arrested for being without certificates: meanwhile those sisters who had courted arrest in vain in the Transvaal were to re-enter Natal. If they were arrested, well and good: if they were not, they were to proceed to the great coal-mining centre of Newcastle to try to persuade the miners—most of them Tamil- or Telugu-speaking Indians—to strike.

I went to Phoenix, and talked to the settlers about my plans. First of all I held a consultation with the sisters living there. I knew that the step of sending these women to jail was fraught with serious risk. Most of them spoke Gujarati. They had not had the training or experience of the Transvaal sisters. Moreover, most of them were related to me, and might act under my undue influence. If afterwards they flinched at the time of actual trial or could not stand the jail, they might be led to apologize, thus not only giving me a deep shock but also causing serious damage to the movement. I decided not to broach the subject to my wife, as she would not say 'no' to any proposal I made, and if she said 'yes', I would not know what value to attach to her assent: and I knew that in a serious matter like this the husband should leave the wife to take what step she liked on her own initiative.

I talked to the other sisters, who readily fell in with my proposal and expressed their readiness to go to jail. They assured me that they would complete their term in jail, come what may. My wife overheard my conversation with the sisters and, addressing me, said, 'I am sorry that you are not telling me anything about this. Why should I be disqualified for the service? I also wish to take the path to which you are inviting others.' 'You know I am the last person to cause you pain,' I replied. 'There is no question of my distrust in you. I would be only too glad if you went to jail, but it should not appear at all as if you went at my instance. In matters like this everyone should act relying solely upon his own strength and courage. I must not prompt you. And then if you began to tremble in the law court or were terrified by hardships in jail, it would be terrible both for you and me, and bad for the cause.' 'You may have nothing to do with me,' she said, 'if being unable to stand jail I secure my release by an apology. If you can endure hardships and also my boys, why cannot I? I must join the struggle.' 'Then I am bound to admit you to it,' said I. 'You know my conditions and you know my temperament. Reconsider the matter if you like, and if after mature thought you deliberately come to the conclusion not to join the movement, you are free to withdraw. There is nothing to be ashamed of in changing your decision even now.'

'I have nothing to think about, I am fully determined,' she said.

I suggested to the other settlers also that each should take his or her decision independently of all others. Again and again, and in a variety of ways I pressed this condition on their attention, that none should fall away whether the struggle was short or long, whether the Phoenix settlement flourished or faded, and whether he or she kept good health or fell ill in jail. All were ready. The only member of the party from outside Phoenix was Parsi

Rustomji, from whom these conferences could not be concealed; and Kakaji, as he was affectionately called, was not the man to lag behind on an occasion like the present. He had already been to jail during the struggle, but he insisted upon paying it another visit.

All went according to expectations. The sisters who had been disappointed in the Transvaal entered Natal but were not challenged at the border. They therefore proceeded to Newcastle and set about their work. Their influence spread like wildfire. The pathetic story of the wrongs heaped up by the £3 tax touched the labourers to the quick, and they went on strike.

Government could now no longer leave the brave Transvaal sisters free to pursue their activities. They were sentenced to imprisonment for three months.

The Women's Part II

The women's bravery was beyond words. They were all kept in the Maritzburg jail, where they were considerably harassed. Their food was of the worst and they were given heavy laundry work as their task. No food was permitted to be given them from outside till nearly the end of their term.

Mrs Gandhi was under a religious vow to restrict herself to a particular diet. After great difficulty the jail authorities allowed her that diet, but the articles supplied were unfit for human consumption. She needed olive oil. She did not get it at first, and when she got it, it was old and rancid. She offered to get it at her own expense but was told that jail was no hotel, and she must take what food was given her. When she was released she was a mere skeleton and her life was saved only by a great effort.

Another returned from jail with a fatal fever to which she succumbed within a few days of her release (22 February 1914). How can I forget her? Valliamma R. Muniswami Mudaliar was a young girl of Johannesburg only sixteen years of age. She was confined to bed when I saw her. As she was a tall girl, her emaciated body was a terrible contrast.

'Valliamma, you are not sorry for having gone to jail?' I asked.

'Sorry? I am even now ready to go again if am arrested,' said Valliamma.

'But what if it results in your death?' I pursued.

'I do not mind. Who would not love to die for one's motherland?' was the reply.

Within a few days after this conversation Valliamma was no more with us in the flesh, but she left us the heritage of an immortal name.

It was an absolutely pure sacrifice that was offered by these sisters. Sacrifice is fruitful only to the extent that it is pure. God hungers after devotion in man. He is glad to accept the widow's mite offered with devotion, without a selfish motive, and rewards it a hundredfold. The unsophisticated Sudama offered a handful of rice, but his heartfelt offering put an end to many years' want and starvation. The imprisonment of many might have been fruitless, but the devoted sacrifice of a single pure soul could never go in vain. None can tell what other sacrifice in South Africa was acceptable to God. But I do know that Valliamma's sacrifice was.

> Valliamma died a martyr on 22 February 1914. Two weeks later, Gandhiji lost his elder brother, Lakshmidas. Even as he grieved, he wrote a letter to Indian Opinion, expressing intense fellow-feeling:
>
> 'To me as a passive resister and as a firm believer in the oneness of the Soul, my brother's loss should occasion no greater pain than the death of Nagappen, Narayanasamy and Hurbatsing, who were just as much my brothers as my blood brother whose loss so many friends are mourning with me. Valliamah Moonsamy's untimely end is, if possible, a greater stab from the hand of Death than my brother's end. Yet, I share the common human failing, and the thoughts that arise in the mind from the loss of my brother, who was in the place of father to me and to whom, next to my dead mother, I owe all I am in life, are more vivid than those that arose in me when those three brother passive resisters and the sister passive resister died.'
>
> (CWMG, Vol. 12, p. 390)

Souls without number spent themselves in the past, are spending themselves in the present and will spend themselves in the future in the service of country and humanity; and that is in the fitness of things as no one knows who is pure. But satyagrahis may rest assured that even if there is only one among them who is pure as crystal, his sacrifice suffices to achieve the end in view. The world rests upon the bedrock of *satya* or truth. *Asatya* meaning untruth literally means *that which is not* as *satya*—truth—also means that which *is*. If untruth does not so much as exist, its so-called victory is death—a negation. And truth being that which *is* can never be destroyed, that is, it is ever victorious. This is the doctrine of satyagraha in a nutshell.

The Labourers Join

The women's imprisonment worked like a charm upon the labourers in the mines near Newcastle who downed their tools and entered the city in successive batches. As soon as I received the news, I left Phoenix for Newcastle.

These labourers had no houses of their own. The mine-owners had built shanties for them, and were responsible for lighting the ways and supplying them with water. Thus they were in a state of utter dependence.

The strikers brought quite a host of complaints to me. Some said the mine-owners had stopped their lights or their water, while others stated that they had thrown away the strikers' household chattels from their quarters. Saiyad Ibrahim, a Pathan, showed his back to me and said, 'Look here, how severely they have thrashed me. I have let the rascals go for your sake, as such are your orders. I am a Pathan, and Pathans never take, but give, a beating.'

'Well done, brother,' I replied. 'I look upon such forbearance as real bravery. We will win through people of your type.'

The labourers were not to be counted by tens but by hundreds. And their number might easily swell into thousands. And it did. How was I to house and feed this ever-growing multitude?

I thought out a solution for my problem. I must take this multitude to the Transvaal and see them safely deposited in jail like the Phoenix party. Their number was about five thousand. I had not the money to pay the railway fare for such a large number of persons, and therefore they could not all be taken by rail. And if they were I would be without the means of putting their morale to the test. The Transvaal border is 36 miles from Newcastle. The border villages of Natal and the Transvaal are Charlestown and Volksrust, respectively. I finally decided to march on foot. I consulted the labourers who had their wives and children with them, and some of whom therefore hesitated to agree to my proposal. I had no alternative except to harden my heart, and declared that those who wished were free to return to the mines. But none of them would avail themselves of this liberty. We decided that those who were disabled should be sent by rail, and all able-bodied persons announced their readiness to go to Charlestown on foot. The march was to be accomplished in two days. In the end everyone was glad that the move was made. The Europeans in Newcastle anticipated an outbreak of plague, and were anxious to take all manner of steps in order to prevent it. By making a move we restored to them their peace of mind and also saved ourselves from the irksome measures to which they would have subjected us.

While preparations for the march were afoot, I received an invitation to meet the coal-owners and I went to Durban: but they would not agree that the £3 tax had anything to do with their mines, and I could not persuade them to petition the Government to take off the tax.

I therefore returned to Newcastle. Labourers were still pouring in from all directions. I clearly explained the whole situation to the men. I said they were still free to return to work if they wished. I told them about the threats held out by the coal-owners, and

pictured before them the risks of the future. I pointed out that no one could tell when the struggle would end. I described to the men the hardships of jail, and yet they would not flinch. They fearlessly replied that they would never be downhearted so long as I was fighting by their side, and they asked me not to be anxious about them as they were inured to hardships.

It was now only left for us to march. The labourers were informed one evening that they were to commence the march early next morning (28 October 1913), and the rules to be observed on the march were read out to them. It was no joke to control a multitude of five or six thousand men. I told them I could not afford to give them anything on the road beyond a daily ration of a pound and a half of bread and an ounce of sugar per head. If possible I would try to get something more from the Indian traders on the way. But if I failed they must rest content with bread and sugar. My experience of the Boer War and the Zulu 'rebellion' stood me in good stead on the present occasion. None of the party was to keep with him any more clothes than necessary. None was to touch anybody's property on the way. They were to bear it patiently if any official or non-official European met them and abused or even flogged them. They were to allow themselves to be arrested if the police offered to arrest them. The march must continue even if I was arrested. All these points were explained to the men and I also announced the names of those who should successively lead the men in place of me.

The men understood the instructions issued to them, and our caravan safely reached Charlestown where the traders rendered us great help. They gave us the use of their houses, and permitted us to make our cooking arrangements on the grounds of the mosque. The ration supplied on the march was just enough for that purpose. At Charlestown we were to halt for some days and therefore were in need of cooking-pots, which were cheerfully supplied by the traders. We had with us a plentiful store of rice and other provisions to which also the traders contributed their share.

Charlestown was a small village with a population of hardly 1,000 souls, and could never accommodate several thousand men. Only women and children were lodged in houses. All the rest camped in the open.

It was very difficult to make our people observe rules of sanitation. But my co-workers lightened my task. It has been my constant experience that much can be done if the leader becomes the chief servant and actually serves and does not dictate to the people. If he puts in bodily labour himself, others will follow him. At least such was my experience on the present occasion. My co-workers and I never hesitated to do sweeping, scavenging and similar work, with the result that others also took it up enthusiastically. If one will not bend one's back to the work, it is no good issuing orders. All would assume leadership and dictate to others and there would be nothing done in the end. But where the leader himself becomes a servant, there are no rival claimants for leadership.

The ration consisted of rice and dal. We had a large stock of vegetables, which could not be cooked separately for want of time and cooking-pots and were therefore mixed with dal. The kitchen was active all the twenty-four hours, as hungry men and women would arrive at any time of the day or night. No labourers were to stop at Newcastle. All knew the way and therefore they used to make for Charlestown directly they left the mines.

As I think of the patience and endurance of the men and women, I am overpowered by a sense of the goodness of God. I was the chief cook. Sometimes there was too much water in the dal, at other times it was insufficiently cooked. The vegetables and even the rice were sometimes ill-cooked. I have not seen many in the world who would cheerfully gulp down such food. On the other hand, I have observed in the South African jails that even those who pass as well-educated men lose their temper if they are given food somewhat less than the rationed quantity or ill-cooked, or even if they get it a little late.

Serving the food was if possible even more difficult than cooking it, and was in my sole charge. I shouldered the responsibility for the food being well- or ill-cooked. Even so it rested with me to satisfy all present by cutting down the individual ration when there was too little food and more than the expected number of diners. I can never forget the angry look which the sisters gave me for a moment when I gave them too little. But it was transformed into a smile when they understood the thanklessness of my self-chosen task. 'I am helpless,' I would say. 'The quantity cooked is small, and as I have to feed an indefinite number I must divide it equally between them.' Upon this they would grasp the situation and go away smiling, saying that they were content.

The Great Trek

1

The time for leaving Charlestown had now arrived. I wrote to the Government that we did not propose to enter the Transvaal with a view to settle there, but as an effective protest against the Minister's breach of pledge and purely as a demonstration of our distress at the loss of our self-respect. The Government would be relieving us of all anxiety if they were good enough to arrest us where we then were, that is, in Charlestown. But if they did not and if any of us surreptitiously entered the Transvaal, the responsibility would not be ours. There was no secrecy about our movement. None of us had an axe to grind. We would not like it if any of us secretly entered the Transvaal, but we could not hold ourselves responsible for the acts of any as we had to deal with thousands of unknown men, and as we could not command any other sanction but that of love. Finally I assured the Government that if they repealed the £3 tax, the strike would be called off and the indentured labourers would return to work, as we would not ask them to join the general struggle directed against our other grievances.

The position therefore was quite uncertain, and there was no knowing when the Government would arrest us. But at a crisis like this we could not wait indefinitely for the reply of the Government. We therefore decided to leave Charlestown and enter the Transvaal by a given date if the Government did not put us under arrest. If we were not arrested on the way, the 'army of peace' was to march twenty to twenty-four miles a day for eight days together, with a view to reach Tolstoy Farm, and to stop there till the struggle was over, and in the meanwhile to maintain itself by working in the farm. Mr Kallenbach had made all the necessary arrangements. The idea was to construct mud huts with the help of the pilgrims themselves. So long as the huts were under construction, the old and the infirm should be accommodated in small tents, the able-bodied camping in the open. The only difficulty was, that the rains were now about to set in, and everyone must have a shelter over his head while it was raining. But Mr Kallenbach was courageously confident of solving it somehow or other.

We also made other preparations for the march. The good Dr Briscoe, the Health Officer of Charlestown, who had been very sympathetic throughout, improvised a small medical chest for us, and gave us some instruments which a layman like myself could also handle. The chest was to be carried bodily as there was to be no conveyance with pilgrims. We therefore carried with us the least possible quantity of medicines, which would not enable us to treat even a hundred persons at the same time. But that did not matter as we proposed to encamp every day near some village, where we hoped to get the drugs of which we ran short, and as we were not taking with us any of the patients or disabled persons, whom we had arranged to leave in the villages *en route*.

Bread and sugar constituted our sole ration, but how was a supply of bread to be ensured on the eight days' march? It must be distributed to the pilgrims every day and we could not hold any of it in stock. The only solution of this problem was that someone should supply us with bread at each stage. But who would be our provider? There were no Indian bakers at all. Again there could not be found a baker in each of the villages, which usually depended upon the cities for their supply of bread. The bread therefore must be supplied by some baker and sent by rail to the appointed station. Volksrust was about double the size of Charlestown, and a large European bakery there willingly contracted to supply bread at each place. The baker did not take advantage of our awkward plight to charge us higher than the market rates and supplied bread made of excellent flour. He sent it in time by rail, and the railway officials, also Europeans, not only promptly delivered it to us, but they took good care of it in transit and gave us some special facilities. They knew that we harboured no enmity in our hearts, intended no harm to any living soul and sought redress only through self-suffering. The atmosphere around us was thus purified and continued to be pure. The feeling of love, which is dormant though present in all mankind had become active. Everyone realized that we are all brothers whether Christians, Jews, Hindus, Mussalmans or anything else.

When all the preparations for the march were completed, I made one more effort to achieve a settlement. I had already sent letters and telegrams. I now telephoned General Smuts. I received this reply within half a minute: 'General Smuts will have nothing to do with you. You may do just as you please.' With this the connection was cut off. I had fully expected this result, though I was not prepared for the curtness of the reply. The next day (6 November 1913) at the appointed hour (6.30 a.m.) we offered prayers and commenced the march in the name of God. The marching column was composed of 2,037 men, 127 women and 57 children.

The Great Trek

11

There is a small spring one mile from Charlestown, and as soon as one crosses it, one enters Volksrust and the Transvaal. A small patrol of mounted policemen was on duty at the border. I went up to them, leaving instructions with my companions to cross over when I signalled to them. But while I was still talking with the police, they made a sudden rush and crossed the border. The police tried to stop them, but the surging multitude was not easy to control. The police had no intention of arresting us. I reasoned with the men and got them to arrange themselves in regular rows. Everything was in order in a few minutes and the march into the Transvaal began.

Two days before this the Europeans of Volksrust had held a meeting where they had offered all manner of threats to us. Some said that they would shoot us if we entered the Transvaal. Mr Kallenbach had attended this meeting to put the Indian case before the Europeans, who were however not prepared to listen to him.

We had heard about this meeting and were prepared for any mischief by the Europeans in Volksrust. It was possible that the large number of policemen massed at the border was intended as a check upon us. However that may be, our procession passed through the place in peace. I do not remember that any European attempted even a jest. All were out to witness this novel sight, while there was even a friendly twinkle in the eyes of some of them.

On the first day we were to stop for the night at Palmford, about eight miles from Volksrust, and we reached the place at about five o'clock in the evening. The men took their ration of bread and sugar, and stretched themselves in the open air. Some were talking while others were singing bhajans. Some of the women were thoroughly exhausted by the march. They had dared to carry their children in their arms but it was impossible for them to proceed further. I therefore, according to my previous warning, lodged them with a good Indian shopkeeper who promised to send them to Tolstoy Farm if we were permitted to reach as far, or to their homes if we were arrested.

As the night advanced, all noises ceased and I was preparing to retire when I heard a tread. I saw a European officer coming, lantern in hand. I understood what it meant, but had no preparations to make. The police officer said:

'I have a warrant to arrest you.'

'When?' I asked.

'Just now.'

'Where will you take me?'

'To the adjoining railway station now, and to Volksrust when we get a train for it.'

'I will go with you without informing anyone, but I will leave some instructions with a co-worker.'

'You may do so.'

I roused P.K. Naidoo who was sleeping near me. I informed him about my arrest and asked him not to awake the others before morning. At daybreak they must regularly resume the march. The march would commence before sunrise, and when it was time for them to halt and get their rations, he must break to them the news of my arrest. He might inform anyone who inquired about me in the interval. If the men were arrested, they must not resist. Otherwise they must continue the march according to the programme. Naidoo had no fears at all. I also told him what was to be done in case he was arrested. Mr Kallenbach was in Volksrust at the time.

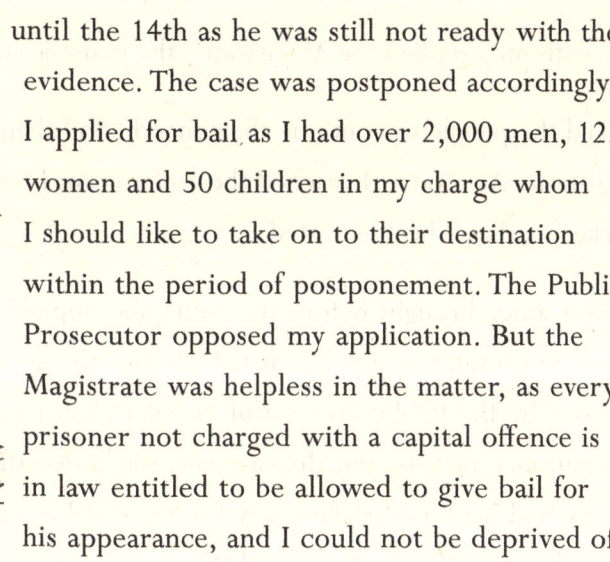

I went with the police officer, and we took the train for Volksrust the next morning. I appeared before the court in Volksrust, but the Public Prosecutor himself asked for a remand until the 14th as he was still not ready with the evidence. The case was postponed accordingly. I applied for bail as I had over 2,000 men, 122 women and 50 children in my charge whom I should like to take on to their destination within the period of postponement. The Public Prosecutor opposed my application. But the Magistrate was helpless in the matter, as every prisoner not charged with a capital offence is in law entitled to be allowed to give bail for his appearance, and I could not be deprived of that right. He therefore released me on bail of £50. Mr Kallenbach had already kept a car ready for me, and he took me at once to rejoin the marchers.

We continued the march, but it could not suit the Government to leave me in a state of freedom. I was therefore re-arrested at Standerton on the 8th. Standerton is comparatively a bigger place. There was something rather strange about the manner of my arrest here. I was distributing bread to the pilgrims. The Indian storekeepers at Standerton presented us with some tins of marmalade, and the distribution therefore took more time than usual. Meanwhile the Magistrate came and stood by my side. He waited till the distribution of rations was over, and then called me aside. I knew the gentleman, who, I thought, perhaps wanted to talk with me. He laughed and said:

'You are my prisoner.'

'It would seem I have received promotion in rank,' I said, 'as magistrates and not mere police officials are now being ordered to arrest me. But you will try me just now.'

'Go with me,' replied the Magistrate, 'the court is still sitting.'

I asked the people to continue their march, and then left with the Magistrate. As soon as I reached the courtroom, I found that some of my co-workers had also been arrested.

I was at once brought before the court and applied for remand and bail on the same grounds as in Volksrust. Here too the application was strongly opposed by the Public Prosecutor and here too I was released on my own recognizance of £50, and the case was remanded till the 21st. The Indian traders had kept a carriage ready for me and I rejoined the company again when they had hardly proceeded three miles further. They thought, and I thought too, that we might now perhaps reach Tolstoy Farm. But that was not to be. It was no small thing however that the men had got accustomed to my being arrested. The five co-workers remained in jail.

We were now nearing Johannesburg. The reader will remember that the whole journey had been divided into eight stages. Thus far we had accomplished our marches exactly according to our programme and we now had four days' march in front of us. But if our spirits rose from day to day, the Government too got more and more anxious as to how they should deal with this Indian invasion. They would be charged with weakness and want of tact if they arrested us after we had reached our destination. If we were to be arrested, we must be arrested before we reached the promised land.

At this time Gokhale sent a cable suggesting that Henry Polak, who had thrown in his lot with us at Phoenix, should go to India and help him in placing the facts of the situation before the Indian and Imperial

Governments. We therefore prepared to send him to India. I wrote to him that he should go. But he would not leave without meeting me in person and taking full instructions. He therefore offered to come and see me during our march. I wired to him, saying that he might come if he wished, though he would in so doing be running the risk of arrest.

Wishing to ask my advice and in spite of the risk of being arrested, Mr Polak joined us on the 9th at Teakworth between Standerton and Greylingstad. We were in the midst of our consultation and it was about 3 o'clock in the afternoon. Polak and I were walking at the head of the whole body of pilgrims. Some of the co-workers were listening to our conversation. Polak was to take the evening train for Durban. But God does not always permit man to carry out his plans. While we were thus engaged in talking, a Cape cart drew up before us and from it alighted Mr Chamney, the Principal Immigration Officer of the Transvaal, and a police officer. They took me aside and one of them said, 'I arrest you.'

I was thus arrested thrice in four days.

'What about the marchers?' I asked.

'We shall see to that,' was the answer.

I said nothing further. I asked Polak to assume charge of and go with the men. The police officer permitted me only to inform the marchers of my arrest. As I proceeded to ask them to keep the peace, etc., the officer interrupted me and said, 'You are now a prisoner and cannot make any speeches.'

I understood my position. As soon as he stopped me speaking, the officer ordered the driver to drive the cart away at full speed. In a moment the men passed out of my sight.

I was taken to Greylingstad, and from Greylingstad *via* Balfour to Heidelberg, where I passed the night.

The caravan with Polak as leader resumed their march and halted for the night at Greylingstad. At about 9 o'clock in the morning of the 10th they reached Balfour, where three special trains were drawn up at the station to take them and deport them to Natal. The men were rather obstinate there. They asked for me to be called and promised to be arrested and to board the trains if I advised them to that effect. But after Mr Polak and Kachhalia Sheth had reasoned with them, pointing out that prison had always been their goal, the pilgrims were brought round and all entrained peacefully.

Triumph of Satyagraha

I was again produced before the Magistrate. This time I had been arrested on a warrant from Dundee and I was therefore taken to Dundee by rail the same day.

Mr Polak was not only not arrested at Balfour but he was even thanked for the assistance he had rendered to the authorities. But he was arrested in Charlestown whilst waiting for the corridor train. Mr Kallenbach was also arrested and both these friends were confined in Volksrust jail.

I was tried in Dundee on the 11th and sentenced to nine months' imprisonment with hard labour. I had still to take my second trial at Volksrust on the charge of aiding and abetting prohibited persons to enter the Transvaal. From Dundee I was therefore taken on the 13th to Volksrust where I was glad to meet Kallenbach and Polak in the jail.

I appeared before the Volksrust Court on the 14th with Polak and Kallenbach. We were each sentenced to three months' imprisonment. We passed a few happy days in Volksrust jail, where new prisoners came every day and brought us news of what was happening outside. Among these satyagrahi prisoners there was one old man named Harbatsinh who was about 75 years of age. Harbatsinh was not working in the mines. He had completed his indenture years ago and he was not therefore a striker. The Indians grew far more enthusiastic after my arrest, and many of them got arrested by crossing over from Natal into the Transvaal. Harbatsinh was one of these enthusiasts.

'Why are you in jail?' I asked Harbatsinh. 'I have not invited old men like you to court jail.'

'How could I help it,' replied Harbatsinh, 'when you, your wife and even your boys went to jail for our sake?'

'But you will not be able to endure the hardships of jail life. I would advise you to secure discharge. Shall I arrange for your release?'

'No, please. I will never leave the jail. I must die one of these days, and how happy should I be to die in jail!'

It was not for me to strive against his unshakable determination. My head bowed in reverence before this illiterate sage. Harbatsinh had his wish and he died in jail on 5 January 1914. His body was with great honour cremated according to Hindu rites in the presence of hundreds of Indians. There was not one but there were many like Harbatsinh in the satyagraha struggle. But the great good fortune of dying in jail was reserved for him alone and hence he is entitled to honourable mention in the history of satyagraha in South Africa.

But to return to the men on the march. The special trains had taken them back to Natal, and there they had immediately been put in prison. The Government had surrounded the mines with fences, declaring them outstations of the Dundee and Newcastle prisons, and put the miners back to work in them. This virtual slavery roused a storm of indignation in India, largely owing to the efforts which Gokhale made although he was very ill. It was then too (December 1913), that Lord Hardinge the Viceroy made his famous speech.

The 'famous speech' was actually made on 24 November 1913 at Madras. Lord Hardinge had said, 'I feel if the South African government desires to justify itself in the eyes of India and the world, the only course open is to appoint a strong impartial committee, whereon Indian interests will be represented, to conduct the most searching inquiry, and you may rest assured that the Raj will not cease to urge these considerations on the Imperial government.'

(CWMG, Vol. 12, p. 603)

It is not usual for the Viceroy to criticize publicly the administration in other parts of the Empire, but upon this occasion Lord Hardinge not only passed severe strictures on the Union Government, but also wholeheartedly defended the action of the satyagrahis. Lord Hardinge's firmness created a profound impression all round. A commission of inquiry was appointed, and although no Indians were among its members, after correspondence with General Smuts I was satisfied that our object could be attained without the continuance of the satyagraha struggle. And sure enough, shortly after the issue of the Commission's report, the Government published in the Official Gazette of the Union the Indians' Relief Bill which was to effect the long-delayed settlement. It abolished the £3 tax, made legal in Africa all marriages that would be deemed legal in India, and made a domicile certificate bearing the holder's thumb-print as sufficient evidence of the right to enter the Union.

Thus the great satyagraha struggle closed after eight years, and it appeared that the Indians in South Africa were now at peace. On 18 July 1914 I sailed for England, to meet Gokhale, on my way back to India, with mixed feelings of pleasure and regret—pleasure because I was returning home after many years and eagerly looked forward to serving the country under Gokhale's guidance, regret because it was a great wrench for me to leave South Africa, where I had passed twenty-one years of my life sharing to the full in the sweets and bitters of human experience, and where I had realized my vocation in life.

Gopal Krishna Gokhale died on 19 February 1915. On 8 May, Gandhiji spoke at a function held in Bangalore for unveiling Gokhale's portrait, where he spelt out his 'vocation in life':

'I have declared myself in the political field and I have him as my Rajya Guru; and this I claim on behalf of the Indian people. It was in 1896 that I made this declaration, and I do not want to regret having made the choice.

'Mr Gokhale taught me that the dream of every Indian, who claims to love his country, should be to act in the political field, should be not to glorify in language, but to spiritualize the political life of the country, and the political institutions of the country.... I have dedicated myself to that ideal.'

(CWMG, Vol. 13, p. 78)